TOGETHER WE *Fly*

VOICES FROM THE DC-3

TOGETHER WE *Fly*

VOICES FROM THE DC-3

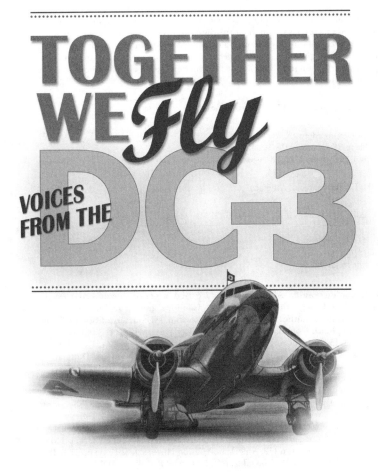

Julie Boatman Filucci

Aviation Supplies & Academics, Inc.
Newcastle, Washington

Together We Fly: Voices From the DC-3
by Julie Boatman Filucci

Published 2011 by Aviation Supplies & Academics, Inc.

Aviation Supplies & Academics, Inc.
7005 132nd Place SE | Newcastle, Washington 98059
Internet: www.asa2fly.com | Email: asa@asa2fly.com

Printed in the United States of America

2014   2013   2012   2011   9   8   7   6   5   4   3   2   1

ASA-DC-3
ISBN   1-56027-865-X
        978-1-56027-865-8

Photo and illustration credits: All photographs are used by permission and courtesy of the copyright owners. Unless otherwise indicated (as follows, and throughout the book) photographs are from the author's collection—photo on p. xv, courtesy of Boeing Douglas Archives (note: all photos from Boeing Douglas Archives are copyright © Boeing); p.3, Bob Knill; p.4, Library of Congress; p.8, MIT Museum; pp.13–16, 20–21, 24–26, Boeing Douglas Archives; pp.31–32, C.R. Smith Museum; pp.34–35, Boeing Douglas Archives; p.35 (of Walt Braznell), C.R. Smith Museum; p.38, C.R. Smith Museum/ American Airlines, Inc.; p.43, American Airlines, Inc.; p.44, Kelly Owen; pp.45, 48, Jeppesen; p.49, Boeing Douglas Archives; p. 51, Zoe Dell Nutter; p.52, C.R. Smith Museum/American Airlines; p.55, Douglas Aircraft via the Scott Thompson Collection; pp.56, 59, 63–67, 72, Boeing Douglas Archives; p.79, Greg Morehead; p.83, U.S.A.F. (from www.af.mil/photos/); p.93, C.R. Smith Museum; pp.93–97, 99, from the Dell Follett Johnson Collection; pp.111–112, Emily Howell Warner; p.113, Julie Clark; p.116, Jay Honeck; p.117, Dan Gryder; p.119, American Aviation Historical Society; pp.123–124, Tyson V. Rininger; p.131, Arnaldo Gonzalez; p.136, Michael P. Collins, AOPA; p.142, C.R. Smith Museum/American Airlines; pp.143, 147, Dan Gryder; p.153, Trevor Morson; p.155, Greg Morehead; pp.156, 158, Jessica Ambats.

Library of Congress Cataloging-In-Publication data:

Filucci, Julie Boatman.
    Together we fly : voices from the DC-3 / Julie Boatman Filucci. — 1st
        p.   cm.
    ISBN-13: 978-1-56027-795-8 (hardback)
    ISBN-10: 1-56027-795-5 (hardcover)
    ISBN-13: 978-1-56027-865-8 (trade paper)
    1. Douglas DC-3 (Transport plane)—Anecdotes.   I. Title.
    TL686.D65F55 2011
    387.7'33430922—dc23
                            2011018122

Contents

~

To Robert Boatman, Hump Pilot,
and to "Darla Dee,"
for always taking care of us

~

"IN AVIATION, AS IN ANY PROGRESSIVE industry, one has to enlarge, in a way soften, the cold facts of practicability."

—Donald Wills Douglas

Foreword

by Jack J. Pelton

A MAN, A VISION, AND A TEAM created an airplane that changed the world in profound ways. *Together We Fly: Voices From The DC-3* is a fitting tribute to capture the far-reaching impact that has made this plane so special for 75 years. But could this plane also be an anchor in a young man's life? I can certainly say it was an anchor in mine. While growing up in Southern California, the DC-3 created a bond for me with my father. It also inspired me to pursue a career in the industry that Donald Douglas made so romantic.

My father, Jack, served in the Army Air Corps as a pilot. He flew many great planes during his time in the service. He soloed in a Ryan PT-22, getting his multi-engine rating in a Cessna T-50 "Bamboo Bomber" and eventually flying the C-47/DC-3 in the Air Transport Command. He had his heart set on flying a Douglas-built plane when he was still attending Bell High School in the suburbs of Los Angeles. His high school sweetheart, eventually his wife and my mother, said that was all he talked about.

In his civilian life he continued to fly. He owned a little Cessna 140A that kept alive his addiction to being in the sky. Family outings were to airshows and aviation events. While most kids had other interests, Dad helped his boys build model airplanes of all types. During those building sessions, he told us many stories about aviation history or specifically about the plane being built at the time. Each plane was unique but none had the place in my dad's heart like the C-47/DC-3.

He would talk constantly about the DC-3's performance. The ability pilots had to land it practically anywhere. The incredible payload it could hold. The structural integrity and clean lines of the Douglas design really captured him. He would say, "If it fit, it went." With his wry Irish grin he would also tell the stories that made you laugh. "You know with a little rudder input you can create a rolling affect that made everyone in the back sick." Even today, next to his reading chair is a model of the legendary DC-3.

By the early 1960s, the jet age had arrived with the DC-8 entering into service. On summer days I would occasionally go to work with my dad. His dental practice was next to the Long Beach Airport. Driving to work, he took Lakewood Boulevard that ran right through the center of the Douglas plant in Long Beach. I was always in awe at this enormous plant. DC-8s, DC-9s, and people everywhere. The Douglas globe at the entrance of the headquarters building and the spectacular neon sign on the DC-8 hangar: "Fly DC Jets." The plant radiated an allure that attracted people on many levels. The coup de grace sealing my fate was a special Saturday morning adventure around 1964. We went as a family to LAX in our Sunday best. The occasion was a "flight to nowhere." This was a chance to take a 30-minute flight in a United DC-8, which Douglas arranged in order to get people comfortable with jet travel. I was in grade school at the time. Having only flown for many hours in the Cessna 140A, this was a big-time thrill. Addictions come in many forms and this was to become mine. I really wanted to be a part of Douglas.

I got my chance while attending college in Long Beach. Douglas hired me, and over the next 21 years I learned what made Douglas products so special. Working in the engineering department with so many of the Douglas pioneers, I got to be a part of something very special. The Douglas team was truly a family. Not only because of the many generations of family members that worked there, but also how they worked so well together with one goal in mind. Tirelessly, they continued the legacy of Donald Douglas' vision in founding the company: Airplanes that would be leaders in their class.

The lunchtime discussions were about continuing the pride of the superior designs Douglas produced. Wings that were aerodynamically the most optimum, no vortex generators or devices needed. Pure art with efficiency. Structure that was the most robust in the industry. If it was going to carry a Douglas employee it had to be the strongest. These were inherent values and part of the unique culture Donald Douglas created. They worked hard, played hard, and took care of each other.

The stories of the culture and products are timeless. How did it anchor me during my inquisitive youth? I think it is best told with a classic Donald Douglas story. One of my "cube mates" at Douglas was the son of an original Douglas Santa Monica executive. He told me about the endless hours the team spent in bringing the DC-3 from concept to reality. His dad had been working around the clock and seven days a week on the project. One evening a delivery came to their home, flowers for his mom with a note. The note was from Donald Douglas, deeply appreciative of her husband's efforts and her sacrifice with him being away from home. This example of authentic leadership forever was etched in my mind. The man, the vision and his exemplary leadership was to set a standard for which the aviation community today can be truly grateful. I know I am.

—Jack J. Pelton
Former Douglas Aircraft Company engineer
CEO, Cessna Aircraft Company (retired)

Preface—Gathering the Voices

A LITTLE MORE THAN SIX YEARS ago, I was handed the opportunity of a lifetime to fly the Douglas DC-3. From that opportunity came an article celebrating the 70th anniversary of the airplane for *AOPA Pilot* magazine. From that article came a response like no other to any article I'd written before. Pilots, mechanics, flight attendants, engineers, soldiers, passengers and spectators wanted to share their relationship with the airplane.

The airplane flies through her 75th year on the wings of those stories. But with the passing of time, the stories lose their voice unless they are put to paper. With this book I hope to preserve a few of those voices. To capture the stories, each chapter starts with a narrative, followed by the story behind the story, and additional details to move the timeline forward.

Interviews conducted during the research for my article, "Douglas DC-3: Together We Fly" [*AOPA Pilot*, December 2005], were used to assist with the creation of this book, as were emails and letters and interviews and visits that followed its publication. My appreciation goes to *AOPA Pilot* magazine for the ability to draw freely from these sources.

—Julie Boatman Filucci
April 2011

Members of the team that created the Douglas DC-1, DC-2, and DC-3 gathered in Santa Monica, California at the ramp of the Douglas Aircraft Company in 1958. From left to right, with their titles at the time of the DC-series, they are: Arthur Raymond (assistant chief engineer), J.L. (Lee) Arnold (design engineer), George Strompl (shop superintendent), Dr. W. Bailey Oswald (Cal Tech physicist and consultant), James H. (Dutch) Kindelberger (chief engineer), Donald W. Douglas (founder and president), Edward F. Burton (design engineer), Franklin R. Collbohm (flight engineer [DC-1], co-pilot [DC-3], and chief of flight research), and Jacob Moxness (test pilot). *(Courtesy of Boeing Douglas Archives)*

Doug

He was desperate to get closer to the rope, to the edge of the field, in front of the orderly rows of civilian spectators lined up to see the U.S. Army's latest advancement—or latest folly, depending on how you looked at it. He knew only in his heart that he had to be closer, had to see the Wrights' flying machine firsthand. Out of the pages of that latest issue of *Aviation*, from a black and white photo on a broadsheet to living color in front of him.

They were just testing the air, those times out at the field before, he thought. Now, in front of the crowd of thousands, they'd put the machine through its paces, for real. A true test. If the machine failed, that failure would only grow the sure obstacles ahead—the obstacles in peoples' minds—the biggest ones of all. *So many skeptics, still; how many around me now? But I know the Wrights can do it—I've seen it with my own eyes!*

The trees at the far end of the field didn't look that tall, but Donald Douglas wondered if they posed an impediment. It still seemed amazing to him that the assemblage of rag and wood he could just make out a hundred yards away would take flight, let alone shoot up in the air with enough purchase to clear their branches. He pushed back the brim of his hat to get a better look, and without thinking, leaned against his mother, who sighed. "Donald, please. You'll see enough, soon enough." She was good to come with him; he'd played hooky before but it was different with your mother as an escort. But she'd encouraged her boys, teaching Doug and his older brother, Harold, the points of sail, and now humoring young Doug's aeronautical dreams.

A man approached the brothers at the machine, said a few words, and then with a nod, went to the engine. *That must be*

Mr. Taylor, priming it up. Sure enough, after looking over the assemblage with its glossy cylindrical tank set high atop the heart of the 25-horsepower motor, he topped it with a little oil from the can, and stepped back with another assent to the brothers. One climbed into the seat and arranged himself, while the other strode out to the left wingtip. Doug thought that was Wilbur flying—*he's the one always tipping his bowler a little more.* Another man approached, carrying two stopwatches around his neck—and from what Doug could see, some apparatus strapped to his leg. He climbed into the seat next to Wilbur. The summer afternoon grew steamy from the rain earlier that day, and Doug shrugged off his coat without taking his eyes off the machine. Yet the man at the controls kept on his suit jacket. *How can he stand it? Guess his mind's on other things.*

The presumed Mr. Taylor stepped out from the engine to the right-hand propeller, and making sober, deliberate eye contact with Wilbur, raised his hands to swing the paddle blade. *One swing! No. Another! No. Again! Well...*then a puff and a cough from the motor made him jump. *Almost!* One more swing, another puff, and a cough, and a cough—and the engine turned over. The people around him cheered, drowning out the motor for a moment. Then in the ensuing lull, he could hear it set up a beat, of sorts. And his heart was pounding along.

The collection of white skirts worn by the women surrounding him swayed just slightly as the air moved languorously around them. White dresses, dark suits, like a line of chess pawns awaiting the first move. Out on the field, the machine rocked a little on its skids, showing the inherent yet undirected energy of a toddler on sugar cookies barely restrained against a mother's unbending stare. Then a tuft of wind picked up, just seemingly as Orville steered the machine more directly into it. And with a throw of the throttle lever, Wilbur commanded the first flight of the day. He kept it near the ground until he gained speed, then entered a gentle climbing turn.

"That's it, old boy!" Doug looked around, not expecting to hear his own words out loud—but the intensity of the moment hit him with a force he couldn't resist.

THE SON OF A BANK CASHIER in Brooklyn, Donald Wills Douglas was born in 1892, and his world was filled with invention and the dynamic changes that those inventions wrought. Douglas was entranced by Navy tradition and legend during his childhood—in fact, he followed his brother Harold to the United States Naval Academy in 1909, where he was nicknamed "Doug" to his brother's

Naval academy grounds
(Courtesy of Bob Knill)

"Big Doug."[1] Here he felt in full force the conflict between his family's history with the Navy and his love for the sea with his building passion for aviation. He sailed during summers as a child and continued to sail throughout his life, but the water never commanded his life's work in the way that aviation inevitably would.

When he was in school at Annapolis, he had a chance to see the Wright brothers demonstrate their 1909 Flyer at Fort Myer, in northern Virginia. The Wrights were performing the required trials for a contract with the United States Army—to secure it they had to prove the machine could maintain an average airspeed of 40 mph during trials, with a bonus ($2,500) to the base payment ($25,000) for each mph that the machine exceeded this average speed—and a penalty for each mph below the benchmark. Other requirements included those involving portability and endurance (one hour aloft with an observer).

He went to view one of the acceptance flights with his mother on July 30, 1909, a day when the Wrights had commissioned an enterprising man by the name of Thomas Edison to film the events there.[2] (Edison's son would become a friend of Douglas' during his college years, and he would later turn down an offer to work for Edison in favor of pursuing a career in aviation.) The day marked the final trial, the time trial, and it was a great success— the Wrights bested the baseline speed by more than 2 mph, secur-

1909 Flyer
(Courtesy of the Library of Congress)

ing a $30,000 payment. Don was 17 years old; all of the excitement undoubtedly impressed the young man.

Earlier that summer, he had seen Glenn Curtiss fly one of his airplanes, the Golden Flier, from Morris Park Race Track on Long Island with his father during a meet hosted by the Aeronautical Society of New York—just as the Wrights and Curtiss became embroiled in a bitter fight over patent infringement. The competitive fire that fueled the aviation industry burned hot in these early years, and that spirit would drive Douglas through his career to develop, time and again, the airplane that would best his competitors—and exceed his customers' expectations.

1. "Sky Master: The Story of Donald Douglas," by Frank Cunningham
2. "Donald W. Douglas: A Heart With Wings," by Wilbur H. Morrison

Doug smoothed back a dark hank of bangs from his forehead as he carefully clipped the article from the journal. He'd searched the newsstands all over Annapolis for any mention of aerodromes, in any obscure rag, until he found one. Snapping it up, he had handed the 12 pennies over to the shopkeeper a bit reluctantly and tucked the journal into his bag before anyone had a chance to see the cover. Inside, he'd felt buoyant, but he stuffed down the laughter and nearly ran the six blocks back to the academy.

Once safely in his room, his roommate gone for the moment, he took the clipping and pasted it into the leather-bound book he'd bought a few days before, after going with his mother to Fort Myer. That's where they saw it, that fantastic machine that now filled his mind. English class was a blur, history a muddle. He sat up straight in maths, though, because it seemed each equation might unlock the mystery of how that machine flew.

He penciled into the margin the date, since he couldn't get that part of the article to cut away neatly from the binding. He sat back and sighed. The scrapbook was pathetically bare, so many blank pages, so little he knew. But he couldn't stop staring at the one picture he'd pasted in after the demonstration, from a flyer he'd carried back from Virginia—of the Wrights launching their ship from a grass field, gaining height, and just dipping into a turn as if it knew how.

The door opened and his roommate blew in, threw his dark wool jacket on the chair, and went into the rain bath. Doug heard the blast as the shower came on, the water beating into the tile. He closed the book and tucked it under his bag on the desk.

Later that night, he grabbed the model that he'd been working on from under his bed, and crept out of the dormitory.
Crossing the grass to the armory, he barely missed the guard
making the rounds. He pulled open the door and it canted on
its hinge to let him in.

Inside, the main hall beckoned. A glow came in through the
windows around the balcony, and the parade floor stretched
out ahead of him in the soft light. He set the model on the
floor, and tried to picture the same rail the Wrights used
nailed down on the floor's hardwood planks. He'd worked it
out that he'd need at least 20 feet of rail to properly guide
the model before it had enough speed to get airborne. Laying
out the rail would take more time than he had tonight, and
he needed some other middie to help. The first launch would
have to wait, but he smiled in the half-dark as he imagined
the little airplane in his hands coasting into the thick air
of the hall.

DOUGLAS TOOK THE INSPIRING SIGHT OF the Wrights' and
Curtiss' flying successes to heart, as well as those of other aeronautical contestants. From his dormitory room, he set upon the
design of several models of his own, which he built and flew on
the common and from his dormitory window. His leather-bound

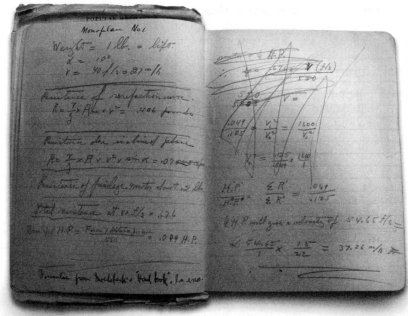

Looking inside
Douglas' scrapbook
opens a window
into the lifelong
passion he had for
aircraft design.

scrapbooks are filled with clippings annotated in pencil, in his broad teenaged hand, the equations for his models carefully derived on the following pages.

In Douglas' handwriting: "Compare the curving of the 'plane' surface of Wright's aerodrome to that of Farmon's machine, and that of Delagray's flyer. Note that Wright's is not so curved as those of the Frenchmen. For comparison select Plate II–XIII, XXI–XIX, XXIII. Plate below illustrates this same fact."

The next pages show his penciled calculations for his "Monoplane 1" model, which are followed by similar pages on the second and third iterations. He would build these models and fly them on the greens outside Bancroft Hall during his precious free time.

His superiors at the naval academy frowned upon Douglas' aeronautical activities, believing that they were a distraction from the maritime studies upon which a good midshipman ("middie") should focus his time. It would be only a few years later that the service saw its first naval aviators, flying from nearby Greenbury Point. By that time, in 1916 and 1917, the academy gave a nod to burgeoning interest in aeronautical engineering and condoned the building of a full-scale flying machine—a glider built by midshipmen Charles Halpine and Colin Headlee. No record survives that it actually flew.

Douglas spent another year at Annapolis, and then his older brother, Harold, graduated. With his emotional ties to the academy fading, he arranged a transfer to the Massachusetts Institute of Technology (MIT) in 1912 to pursue mechanical engineering (the closest discipline available at the time). He would soon become one of MIT's first students of aeronautical engineering: Jerome Hunsaker led the new department, formally begun in 1914, and became Douglas' mentor.

Later in 1914, Douglas graduated, after two years at the school, and his first position was continuing to work with Hunsaker as an assistant professor of aeronautical engineering. A primary project: Hunsaker, Douglas, and the budding department developed the school's new wind tunnel, to replace an original model built in 1896.

This first Hunsaker wind tunnel measured four feet square, and it was constructed from wood and metal, housing a model on a pedestal in the center of the apparatus. The wind tunnel allowed engineers to test their designs prior to launching them into the

skies. While this concept sounds obvious even to a lay person to-day, only after several years of trial and error (sometimes with fatal results) did the nascent aviation industry have the critical tool it needed to properly test designs. The original tunnel served until 1920, when a circular tunnel, four feet in diameter, was built, followed by subsequently larger tunnels.

His scholarship complete, Douglas was eager to jump into the industry. Hunsaker helped him secure a job as a consultant at the Connecticut Aircraft Company in 1915, but he soon was ready to move onward. Again, his choice of mentor proved fortunate: On Hunsaker's letter of recommendation, Douglas traveled to Los Angeles to join Glenn L. Martin's company as chief engineer. He held that position for a year, and in November 1916, he joined the Army Signal Corps in Washington, D.C. as chief civilian aeronautical engineer. He'd married Charlotte Marguerite Ogg by this time. He spent a year working with the government to improve its airplanes, but as a person destined to lead rather than follow, he chafed at the bureaucracy.

In 1918 Martin offered him employment again when he opened a plant in Cleveland, Ohio, and Douglas accepted. His first task was to lead the design of Martin's new twin-engine bomber. During his second time at Martin, he met Eric Springer, a pilot who would eventually join Douglas in his own company. Douglas and the team at Martin adapted the Martin Twin to carry passengers, a choice that helped Martin stay afloat financially after the end of World War I, and foreshadowed a key direction that Douglas would eventually take in his career: commercial civilian aviation.

Life in Cleveland didn't suit the growing Douglas family (two sons, Donald, Jr., born in 1917, and William, born in 1918), and in March 1920 Douglas concluded that the family would move permanently to southern California. With the move, he would also make another life-changing decision—to found his own aircraft company. Douglas was just turning 28, but he had accumulated a wealth of diverse experience—and the stature in the still-small industry—necessary to propel him through this bold step.

Douglas left Martin amicably and set out to find the financial support he needed to get the company started. His connections led him to affluent sportsman David R. Davis, of Los Angeles, who was interested in investing in an airplane that would cross the United States nonstop. The Davis-Douglas Airplane Company was incorporated in June 1920; soon, Douglas invited several former colleagues from Martin to join him in California—including George Strompl, who would go on to become Douglas' first plant manager and remained a senior official at the company for his career.

Douglas had a keen interest in the value of the airplane for commercial use that he sought to develop. When Douglas left Martin, the airplane was still viewed as primarily an instrument of the military, with limited use in cargo-carrying applications, and even more limited utility in passenger-carrying operations. Those limitations stemmed from three critical problem areas: dispatch reliability, passenger comfort, and avoiding the inherent hazards associated with flying aircraft following World War I.

But Douglas rightly predicted that advances in aeronautical engineering gained through the military application of the airplane would soon offer safety "comparable with that of our present means of travel"—the railroad—and that passengers would pay twice the train fare to reduce travel time in half. "The first problem, then, seems to be to win the confidence of the public," writes Douglas in 1919 in an article for the journal of The Society of Automotive Engineers, "The Airplane as a Commercial Possibility." (Aeronautical engineering was included in this society from its inception, with the term "automotive" describing any self-propelled vehicle.)

THE AIRPLANE AS A COMMERCIAL POSSIBILITY

By D W Douglas[1]

The factors included in the commercial airplane problem are the practical use that can be made of airplanes, the volume of business that can be expected, the necessary changes from present military types to make an efficient commercial airplane and what the future holds for this new means of transportation. The requirements for passenger transportation, airmail and general express service, are first discussed in detail, consideration then being given to other possibilities such as aerial photography and map-making, the aerial transportation of mineral ores, sport and miscellaneous usage. Changes in the present equipment of engines and airplanes to make them suitable for commercial use are outlined, and special features of aerial navigation, landing fields and legal questions are mentioned.

Douglas' article in the journal of The Society of Automotive Engineers, 1919

According to Douglas, "...few of the airplanes developed for military purposes hold much promise of successful adaptation to peace-time commercial uses," yet he felt strongly that passenger-carrying operations would provide the greatest potential profit because of the human connection they would make possible. "Correspondence, telephony, and telegraphy cannot supply the complete satisfaction of actual personal contact."

In the article, Douglas outlines the requirements that must be met in order for commercial air travel to be sustained profitably—demonstrating that not only was he an astute engineer, but his grasp of which results mattered to make a sound business plan enabled him to see the big picture clearly. "Assuming larger and faster land machines working up to the limit of their capacity, it can be shown that passengers can be carried at a good profit as low as 10 cents per passenger-mile." The "larger and faster land machine" to which Douglas referred to was a multi-engine land airplane carrying at least 8 passengers at 100 mph—state of the art in 1919.

Innately frugal, Douglas was throughout his life attuned to the bottom line, though not in such a way as to put research and development investment at the mercy of the numbers. This clarity of purpose fueled his ability to lead his company to success.

Barbershop Days

The close air carried the sweet smell of bay rum and lime. A track of sweat coursed its way down the young man's cheek as he bent over the makeshift table, just a sheet of wood laid over two sawhorses. Though it tickled as it hit his upper lip, he didn't move to wipe it, but continued with his pencil line on the curling, onionskin paper. Opposite him at the table worked another man, thinning hair slicked back with dressing, and in need of a cut from the boys clipping away just beyond the cotton curtain in the shop out front.

Douglas unbuttoned the cuffs of his pressed white oxford and pushed them up without taking his eyes off the plan. Davis' design needed translation to working plans, and before him lay a particularly sticky section—how to assemble the wing in the limited factory space in the second-floor mill shop he'd just paid first months' rent on. Managing the materials was one thing, but accounting for an entire assembly—and getting it out of the shop in large enough pieces to reduce the burden of assembly was the puzzle he was trying to solve.

Davis, it's a good thing that each of these sections isn't that big, he thought as he methodically rubbed out a line on the translucent paper, leaving rolled bits of the spent eraser behind. He thought about the wood lines of the ship's hull, like the hull of a custom boat. So beautiful, but each individual rib is its own size—an oddball. We'll measure it out the best we can on this first model—but down the road we need to know how to standardize it and make it quick to reproduce.

A stocky man lifted the curtain to enter the room; his hairline made him look older than his mid-twenties. Douglas raised his head. "How does it look?" George Strompl almost let a smile crack his face. "The space is good, sir—and there's a spot in the wall in that old carpenter's shop between the beams that we can open up. We'll be able to pass the assemblies through there, I figure." An earthquake had rumbled through the barbershop right after they'd stepped into it for the first time, and Strompl still expected one to shake the floor at any time.

As if he read Strompl's thoughts, Douglas smiled. "One hurdle down...only a thousand more to go." And then the final hurdle, to load it up on the truck, roll it out on the airfield across town and see it fly.

DOUGLAS HAD ITCHED TO SET OFF on his own, but he needed to find a suitable place for the fledgling Davis-Douglas Aircraft Company to start design and production.

Upon arrival in California, he searched for inexpensive space to rent—but it was hard to come by the right combination that would allow for the design and engineering functions to work alongside the manufacturing. His search led him to a building on Pico Boulevard in Los Angeles, which housed a barber shop in the front. The office space was adequate for engineering and company administration, but the assembly of aircraft would have to take place on the second floor of a mill shop nearby, and later at the Goodyear airfield in East Los Angeles.

George Strompl arrived on July 20, 1920, as one of the first five Douglas employees. (Rounding out the five were Ross Elkins, Jim Goodyear, George Borst, and Henry Guerin, who became factory manager at the Santa Monica plant.) Strompl started as purchasing agent, and as noted before, he would stay on Douglas' team for decades. Eric Springer, former Martin chief test pilot, was another early employee of Douglas Aircraft Company, later becoming Douglas' manager at the El Segundo plant near the present-day site of Los Angeles International Airport. Harry Wetzel, also on board from shortly after Douglas started the company, would become Douglas Aircraft Company's general manager and remain there until his death in 1940. That Douglas inspired such long-term loyalty amongst his team was a critical ingredient to the success of the company and to the success of Douglas aircraft designs. He would breed this into his engineering teams in particular. They persevered together because there was respect between them that ran deep.

Copyright© Boeing

Original plant on Wilshire Blvd., interior and exterior
(Photos courtesy of Boeing Douglas Archives)

Copyright© Boeing

The first aircraft they built together was *The Cloudster*, a biplane with a wingspan of 56 feet. Two fuel tanks held a total of 660 gallons and could be jettisoned from the airplane, and the oil tank for the Liberty 400-hp engine held 50 gallons. Springer, who served as test pilot on the airplane, also gave it the name when he said to Douglas, after looking over the plans, "You've got a real cloud duster there, Doug." The first test flight at Goodyear field didn't go

The Cloudster *(Courtesy of Boeing Douglas Archives)*

so well, however, and Springer ground-looped into a cauliflower bed. On the next try a few days later (on February 24, 1921, with Davis also on board) the takeoff was a success. *The Cloudster* stayed in flight for 30 minutes.

Springer set an altitude record in the airplane, but the record-setting transcontinental flight hoped for by Davis and planned for that summer hit the ropes over Texas with a stripped timing gear on the Liberty engine. Eventually *The Cloudster* was beaten to the record by a Fokker T-2. Without the incentive to be first across the country, sportsman Davis lost interest and withdrew from aviation, and Douglas incorporated the Douglas Aircraft Company in December 1921.

Just after *The Cloudster*'s failed transcontinental bid, Douglas secured a government contract for three DT-1 torpedo airplanes. The former company had moved both manufacturing and offices into hangar space at Goodyear field, and though more convenient than the barbershop and mill, the hangar setup still lacked the open floor plan necessary for a true factory. He foresaw more contracts, and the growth that accompanied them, so Douglas located a large vacant building on Wilshire Boulevard in Santa Monica, an abandoned film studio surrounded by empty land, that would suit those needs.

In 1922, in the new Santa Monica plant, Douglas Aircraft Company produced six airplanes. The Douglas family also grew: Douglas' daughter, Barbara Jean, was born November 25, 1922.

**Women covering a
Douglas World Cruiser**
*(Courtesy of Boeing
Douglas Archives)*

The DT-1 had evolved into the DT-2, with a radiator on the nose instead of on the sides. It had a 50-foot wingspan and its top speed was nearly 100 mph. It used another 400-hp Liberty engine. A variant, the DT-4, was used for bombing and had a 650-hp engine.

In the summer of 1923, the Army contracted with Douglas to build four airplanes that would be capable of circling the globe. Work started on the airplanes in the fall, with completion in March 1924 for first flights. The airplanes had both land and water landing gear configurations, and Douglas christened them World Cruisers. Wingspan was 50 feet, and maximum gross weight in the land configuration was 6,915 pounds, and 8,000 pounds in the seaplane configuration.

The logistics established for the round-the-world flights were extensive, but the four ships—the *Boston, Chicago, Seattle,* and *New Orleans*—still faced great objective hazards. Only two airplanes that started would complete the journey (the *Chicago* and the *New Orleans*) and two were lost (the *Seattle* and the *Boston*). The *Seattle* struck a mountainside in Alaska, and the *Boston* had an oil pump failure while en route to Iceland and landed safely on the water—only to capsize during the tow back to shore. (A replacement ship for the *Boston* completed the last portion of the trip.) But all four crew members from the ill-fated pair survived their respective ordeals. In the meantime, Douglas secured another military contract for 50 observation and cargo airplanes—and by January 1925, employment at Douglas Aircraft Company soared to 500 people.

Over the next seven years, Douglas Aircraft Company solidified its reputation as a reliable aircraft manufacturer, producing 162 O-38 observation airplanes for the Army and 59 mail planes (the Douglas M-2) for the U.S. Post Office and for cargo airlines. The Douglas Ambassador was developed as an upscale sportsman's airplane, but it wasn't successful. In fact, Douglas and Springer had an accident in one of the airplanes when the engine failed on takeoff. Though the pair were not seriously injured, the airplane was destroyed, and this incident undoubtedly affected the airplane's sales.

But the dream remained within Douglas to build the viable passenger transport airplane he foresaw in college. Towards this end, the Douglas Dolphin was conceived to help crack the commercial market. This amphibious airplane sold well enough to recoup the investment in it after a handful of wealthy individuals bought cus-

Douglas Dolphin *(Courtesy of Boeing Douglas Archives)*

Original factory site now is Douglas Park, at 26th and Wilshire.

tom-built models. Moreover, the 59 Dolphins that made up the fleet boosted the Douglas reputation for aircraft built to last.

As Santa Monica grew up around the plant on Wilshire, Douglas needed room for expansion. The company purchased land at the Santa Monica Airport in 1927, and the factory moved operations there in 1929. Land adjacent to the original factory site on Wilshire was dedicated as a community park, Douglas Park, at 26th and Wilshire, that is still lovely and well-used today. The Douglas family continued to expand—twin sons, James and Malcolm, were born in 1931.

The Sum of Its Parts

Arthur pushed his glasses up the bridge of his nose and looked up with a sigh from the plans in front of him. There was something about the new gear system on the DC-1 that just wasn't working as well as the young engineer who had inspired it had hoped, now that the airplane was flying. The complex mechanism meant the equivalent of patting your head and rubbing your stomach—with a third hand necessary to fly the airplane. The airplane could require two pilots but certainly not a third just for gear retraction and extension.

He walked out of his office and over to an area of evenly-spaced desks on the open floor where the core of the Douglas engineering team worked as though to an imperceptible metronome. A man here and there at each desk, and one man leaned over sheets of blue-lined prints with a colleague, gesturing into the air with a slim pencil. A couple of years ago, each man had carried his own desk over from the old offices on Wilshire, happy to put a shoulder to the effort in the move, each man an individual but the team greater than the sum of its parts.

They'd put that same effort into their response to the contract from TWA for the airplane he had on his mind. All around the table, over weeks of discussion, each engineer put a voice to the answer to Frye's proposal. They could do a twin-engine plane, they could make the takeoff requirements on one engine, and most important, they could solve the riddle of making passengers happy enough with the experience to come back and fly again.

One of the men looked up and saw Arthur walking by, smiled, and went back to the conversation. Arthur's quiet countenance didn't invite ancillary chit chat, but the respect and warmth he felt amongst the team was genuine. There was no hiding anything from him—perceptive as a Geiger counter, that man—but they didn't really want to. His was the mind that helped them solve problems, not a scared suit that wanted to sweep those problems under the mat. Just like his boss, Dutch.

He looked around the room and was proud of the quiet purpose, and proud that these men had jobs. It had been a roller coaster over the past four years, with the stock market crash, and the fallout that seemed to continue on like aftershocks from an earthquake that would never end. The government had cut back their contracts, making everyone nervous as cats, for good reason. They were so fortunate that Mr. Douglas had more cards in his hand than just that one signed by Washington.

More so than that, there was the vision: to create a real market out of the fits and starts of commercial air service. The Ford Trimotor, the Curtiss Condor, the Boeing 247—they paved the way, and each had its good points, with the 247 being closest to the goal thus far. But none would ring the bell the way that he knew to his bones their ship would.

He thought back to the trip he made out to New York to meet with the TWA folks in the beginning. The cold had soaked his bones as he sat in his seat on the way back on the airline's Ford Trimotor, which then rattled in a beat with the engines. He'd sneezed, popping out the earplugs the young attendant had given him. He had looked over his shoulder—she was huddled in the back of the corrugated box bobbing through the sky, a blanket wrapped around her as she fought to keep her fingers working in thin gloves. The seat would have felt rigid and hard in a schoolhouse, the rattan creaking in the cold—the creaking he felt more than heard as his ears strained in the din.

The sign on the wall stated the Douglas mission clearly—the words written by Douglas himself: "When you design it, think how you would feel if you had to fly it! Safety first!" Safety was the key, the bedrock. Safety would win over a public made wary by crash headlines. And comfort, for both pilots and passengers, would win their hearts. Arthur went back to his desk, sat down, and added a new line to the drawing.

Arthur Raymond grew up in California, and attended the Massachusetts Institute of Technology, as Douglas had, before returning to Los Angeles. He took a job as a metal fitter in the machine shop at Douglas Aircraft Company in 1923—and when Douglas was searching for MIT grads with whom to build his engineering team, he looked no further than the tall, slim Raymond.

Arthur Raymond
*(Courtesy of Boeing
Douglas Archives)*

According to James Douglas, "Dad said you could trust anything Arthur Raymond said implicitly."

The Depression had taken its toll on the aircraft industry, but Douglas Aircraft Company had survived through careful financial management and the strength of the Dolphin and the PD-1 flying boat, among other models. Douglas insisted that development costs for each model had to be written off each year—even if that meant lower dividends for stockholders. (The company had gone public in November 1928.) He didn't want to continue to rely on military contracts, however, knowing how they could come and go with a change in the wind.

Other sweeping changes took place in 1929, when Walter Brown, postmaster general, launched an investigation that determined that airlines would never grow into passenger travel as long as carrying the heavily-subsidized mail was more profitable. The pound-per-mile rate was eliminated, and the McNary-Watres Bill was soon passed, which offered rewards to airlines purchasing transport aircraft. As a result, many smaller airlines went out of business.

One that was left standing was Transcontinental and Western Airlines (TWA), formed by the merger of Western Air and Transcontinental Air Transport in 1930. Jack Frye, vice-president of flight operations, also recognized the need to move the industry toward a passenger-carrying model. On August 2, 1932, Douglas received a letter from Frye (also sent to Martin, Consolidated, Curtiss-Wright, Sikorsky, and General Aviation). That letter, which

Letter to Douglas from Jack Frye
(Courtesy of Boeing Douglas Archives)

TRANSCONTINENTAL & WESTERN AIR INC.
10 RICHARDS ROAD
MUNICIPAL AIRPORT
KANSAS, CITY. MISSOURI

August 2nd,
19 32

Douglas Aircraft Corporation,
Clover Field,
Santa Monica, California.

Attention: Mr. Donald Douglas

Dear Mr. Douglas:

Transcontinental & Western Air is interested in purchasing ten or more trimotored transport planes. I am attaching our general performance specifications, covering this equipment and would appreciate your advising whether your Company is interested in this manufacturing job.

If so, approximately how long would it take to turn out the first plane for service tests?

Very truly yours,

Jack Frye

Jack Frye
Vice President
In Charge of Operations

JF/GS
Encl.

N.B. Please consider this information confidential and return specifications if you are not interested.

SAVE TIME — USE THE AIR MAIL

Copyright © Boeing

THE SUM OF ITS PARTS

21

Douglas later referred to as the "birth certificate of the modern airliner," outlined TWA's proposal for the purchase of "10 or more trimotored transport airplanes."

The aircraft specifications outlined in the letter called for a maximum gross weight of 14,000 pounds, a range of 1,000 miles, the capacity to carry 12 passengers and two pilots, and the ability to take off fully loaded with two of the three engines in operation—essentially, after one engine failed on takeoff. After the Douglas engineering team developed a proposal, Arthur Raymond, who had been promoted to assistant chief engineer, and Harold Wetzel, the general manager, boarded a train for New York to present their plan to TWA.

"We traveled by train for two reasons," said Raymond. "We had much ground to cover and hundreds of details to lay out, and I needed secluded time to work out my performance figures. Also, we really wanted to get there."[1]

Raymond made the trip home on a TWA Ford Trimotor. He knew what TWA was looking for—something like the Ford Trimotor, but better. When Raymond boarded the aircraft, nicknamed the "Tin Goose," he received the usual "comfort pack," which included cotton for his ears, smelling salts for if he felt faint, and an airsick cup.

The trip radically changed Raymond's idea of what to design. What came off the Douglas drawing board was a twin-engine, low-wing, all-metal monoplane—not the metal box that essentially formed the Tin Goose. The engineers decided not to use electrical gear retraction (as in the Boeing 247) since they felt the apparatus was subject to failure. Instead, the gear would be hydraulically activated, and retract into the newly-developed NACA streamlined nacelles.

That airplane would become the DC-1.

1. "The Legacy of the DC-3," by Henry Holden

Devil in the Details

A first flight meant short and simple. Confirm the basic airworthiness of the prototype and, thus, the design, and identify and contain any problems for later exploration. Carl Cover not only knew this, but in a way cherished the process, the challenge. As he walked out to the DC-1, shiny and new on the ramp outside of the main production hangar at Clover Field, he barely saw the crowd of Douglas employees standing in anticipation of the big moment. More than 800 people, some still snacking on sandwiches from sack lunches. A woman snapped on an apple just within Cover's earshot and it seemed to break his focus for a moment as it cut through the air that July morning. But his mind slid quickly back to the task in front of him.

Run up the engines one last, thorough time; check the systems as best he could while on the ground; signal to his ground crew that he was ready; and make a final consultation with Fred Herman, an assistant engineer riding along as an observer, before taking the DC-1 into the sky for the very first time.

Douglas was nowhere to be seen. He was probably staked out somewhere with Raymond.

The engines were warm from two hours of test run when he started them again, to ensure every nook and cranny of the big Wright 1820s held precious drops of that liquid gold: oil. Still, he ran the airplane up and down the runway, going over each element in the cockpit again and again. Feeling the controls in his hands. Scanning the gauges for any sign of trouble. Testing that wind with her wingtips and tailfeathers. Then the time came for takeoff, for real.

The girl was a ready partner—but he didn't trust her yet. They'd barely met.

So when the left engine stumbled as he pitched into the climb after lifting off from the Santa Monica pavement, coming through 100 feet, Cover was spring-loaded to action. He held the controls with a steady hand and gently leveled off, and the engine coughed its way back to life. He sighed in relief, and eased back again to continue the climb.

Then both engines sputtered.

This was not the emergency he expected. He puzzled through ideas briskly, testing one input for its result, and measuring his success by either engine's continued combustion, and altitude gained or lost. Herman could only look on, questioning just as much as Cover. The ocean frothed a cold blue beneath them.

Carl Cover
(Courtesy of Boeing Douglas Archives)

Striking the balance—climb and sputter, level and fire—he nursed the airplane to 1,200 feet and gently turned back to the field, coming over the large open field nearby just in case. He turned on final, and if he wasn't so tightly focused he could have almost heard the intake of breath on the ground from his colleagues watching. No wonder Doug had been too keyed up to come onto the ramp. He must have pulled out the binoculars for this one—the man must have had a premonition.

But Cover had no room in his mind for all that. The one landing to come was the one that counted more than any other in his career.

He nailed it.

As it turned out, the problem that Carl Cover (Douglas' chief pilot and vice president of sales) encountered on that first flight of the DC-1 was relatively simple and easy to fix—though it stopped the collective Douglas heart when it manifested itself in the air. The Wright Cyclone radial engines had experimental carburetors with the floats hinged at the rear of the assembly. When Cover put the DC-1 into a climb, the carburetors tipped back as well, the action of the float closing the valve and shutting off the supply of gas to the engines. A quick fix to hinge the float at the carburetor's front solved the problem. Aside from this issue,

DC-1 cockpit and exterior
(Courtesy of Boeing Douglas Archives)

there were no other major squawks or concerns with the airplane, though some initial fishtailing was corrected with an adjustment to the rudder linkage and additional rudder surface area. The DC-1 continued to perform according to expectations for 200 hours as the engineering team put it through its paces.

During these extensive tests, Douglas Aircraft Company engineers developed comprehensive performance charts for the airplane that would allow pilots to make precise calculations of parameters such as expected fuel burn and runway length required for takeoff and landing. The result? They could fly more efficiently. With this Douglas unlocked another key to providing a successful commercial air transport—the ability to use time and resources better than the next guy.

"DC" stands for "Douglas Commercial," Douglas' vision come to life. The DC-1's development cost would total more than $800,000—well over Douglas' original estimate of $250,000.

Douglas Aircraft Company would deliver only one DC-1 to TWA, for $125,000—at first blush, a gross miscalculation of return on investment.

But TWA also held a one-year option on 60 more aircraft, at a price of $58,000 each. Both companies determined that, while the DC-1 was a success, there was so much more they could do. So they agreed that Douglas would build the DC-2 to fill the gap.

The DC-2 specifications called for the cabin to be lengthened by three feet to accommodate up to 14 passengers. A copilot's instrument panel was installed, and the landing gear system improved, along with the addition of hydraulically-powered brakes and an autopilot. A new contract was signed for 25 DC-2s, for a total of $1,625,000. Douglas would eventually hold orders for 192 DC-2s. While pilots complained that it was stiff legged, leaky, and somewhat prone to gear failure, it represented a giant leap forward in the airlines' capability to carry passengers safely. Douglas was awarded the Collier Trophy in 1935 for the accomplishment.

And it paved the way for the true queen of the skies.

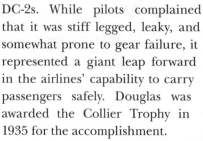

DC-2 cockpit and exterior
(Courtesy of Boeing Douglas Archives)

Copyright© Boeing

TOGETHER WE *Fly* VOICES FROM THE DC-3

Douglas absentmindedly hummed a few bars of the old Scots tune to himself as he stared out the window from his desk. It had been a great trip—the whole family around Europe that May. Too bad the twins were too young to go along. He smiled at the thought of them in rooms full of armor! He took off his round-lensed eyeglasses and set them on the notepad in front of him. The production of the DC-2 was humming along, and he considered the other contracts on his plate—observation planes, for the most part. Bread and butter...

What next? He always wondered, what next?

A knock on the door. "Mr. Douglas?" Vada's voice came through the door a little gruff.

"Yes, Miss Baldwin, come in." She opened the door just a crack. "Mr. Smith from American Airlines is calling. Shall I put him through?"

He lifted an eyebrow. "Certainly, Miss Baldwin." This could be interesting. The airline held orders on fifteen DC-2s, and they'd put a couple on their Chicago–Newark route. He also knew that the post office had recently expanded their contracts with the airline on the southern airmail routes. Maybe he'd sell a few more of the ladies today.

Vada patched C.R. through. "Douglas."

"Mr. Douglas, C.R. Smith here, American Airlines."

Leave it to C.R. to cut straight to the chase, that high Texas drawl not slowing him down one morsel. American had been flying the DC-2s, but C.R. needed something with more room. He wants to replace the Condors—American's sleeper ships—and the narrow -2 just won't do it.

C.R. gave other reasons: The DC-2 wasn't stable in the air, it was stiff-legged and hard to land, and the hand pump to lower the gear and the flaps? That *had* to go. Plus that vision of his about sleepers, that people would pay more to cross the country in the luxury of their own little bedroll in the sky. C.R. had already put his chief engineer, Bill Littlewood, on it. They had plans. They wanted to widen the airplane enough to fill it with fourteen bunks. Or 21 seats, perhaps, should they deign to put it into daytime service.

He just didn't buy it. However was it going to work?

Still, he liked the man from Minerva. He had heard of C.R.'s dependability and integrity. And the one time they were at a meeting together around other American employees, he liked the way he treated his folks, calling them by their first names, and expecting them to call him by his.

But the man could *talk*! Doug pushed back a white cuff to look at his watch. For crying out loud, he'd spent nearly two hours on the phone with him! He smiled. This call was going to cost C.R. a fortune.[1]

"Okay, C.R., let's make a deal. We'll try this errand of Littlewood's, but only at 20 firm orders." A moment of silence as Smith calculated the total. A risk, but Douglas knew sometimes that risk was what it took.

"Let's do it."

~

CYRUS ROWLETT SMITH WAS A straightforward man who did know his employees by name when he was out flying with them on the line. His open countenance, quick smile and a laugh—in Donald Douglas' words, C.R. had "boundless energy." But he was not going to take "no" for an answer when he made the call to Douglas suggesting that the Douglas Aircraft Company, already financially stretched after its implementation of the DC-2 line—Douglas wouldn't invest in tooling until absolutely necessary—go the DC-2 one better for American's proposed sleeper service.

C.R. Smith
(Courtesy of C.R. Smith Museum)

C.R. had really launched his career in the airline industry when he became general manager for Texas Air Transport in 1928. In 1929, TAT (by then renamed Southern Air Transport), was bought by AVCO and transitioned to American Airways. Smith was appointed general manager of American's southern division in 1932.

Fallout from the distribution of air mail contracts in 1930 (known as the 1930 Spoils Conference, as it was viewed that certain airlines unfairly benefited from the closed-door meetings hosted by Brown to assign those contracts) meant that anyone who had attended was essentially barred from heading a major airline. The Air Mail Act of 1934 made this official, and set the stage for the ascension of both Jack Frye, of TWA, and Smith, who became president of American Airlines, the newly created version of American Airways (another condition of the Air Mail Act, prohibiting companies that had benefited from unfair bidding from holding future contracts).

William Littlewood, American's vice-president of engineering, was appointed by Smith to his management team, and charged

The American Airlines team, including Walt Braznell, standing, fourth from right, Bill Littlewood, sitting, first from right, with C.R. Smith to his right.
(Courtesy of C.R. Smith Museum)

$335.50

with outlining the airline's requirements for a new sleeper design based on the DC-2 and the Curtiss Condor. On July 8, 1935, Douglas received the telegram from Smith that placed an order for ten "Model DST transport airplanes" for $795,000 — and that American would have an exclusive on the DST concept until those aircraft were delivered. Smith needed financing, so he reserved the right to reduce the order to eight airplanes if he couldn't secure adequate funding within the month. He also reserved the right to specify that a number of the aircraft actually be "day planes."

Arthur Raymond had responded to Bill Littlewood's suggestions to the design with Douglas Aircraft Report No. 1004. Raymond and his team of Douglas engineers had reviewed Littlewood's specs, and figured they could use roughly 80% of the DC-2 design in the new model. Still, as they dove into the development, the airplane began to evolve.

However, final specs would not arrive until November 14, 1935, and the final contract was not completed until April 8, 1936 — well after the first airplanes went into production. In fact, American accepted the first DST just a couple of weeks later, on April 29, in Phoenix, Arizona, to save the airline from paying the sales tax in California.

Douglas engineers at the time included Harold Adams (who did major design work on the landing gear—with a foundation gained by the team on the development and field experience with the Dolphin's retractable landing gear); Jack Northrop, who created the multicellular wing design; and Dr. W. Bailey Oswald, who contributed further on wing design. Raymond's team would design into the DC series aircraft innovative approaches to retractable landing gear, wing flaps, the stressed-skin structure and flush riveting. The DST was the first commercial airplane delivered with constant-speed propellers, which could also be feathered (twisted to streamline with the oncoming airflow) in the case of an engine failure.

And the development team was not limited to Douglas engineers: Raymond had worked with Littlewood and his assistant Otto Kirchener on the specs even before the final specifications were sent, even before the contract for the aircraft was set down.

"We gave Bill (Littlewood) almost a free hand in establishing the dimensions in the cabin and deciding what went into the cockpit layout," said Raymond. "The DC-3 was a product of teamwork. This was the primary reason it was so successful."[2]

Dr. W. Bailey Oswald
(Courtesy of Boeing Douglas Archives)

Oswald describes the process by which they changed the airfoil after many wind tunnel tests: "We tried dozens of models in the wind tunnel before we hit on the secret. We narrowed the airfoil, which changed the center of balance of the airplane resulting in the final wing design being enormously strong."[3] The cantilever wing design was a pretty new concept, but truly different was the use of smooth aluminum skin over corrugated aluminum underneath—riveted together under compression, creating strength greater than the sum of the two sheets.

Passenger comfort was key, as well, and both Douglas and American engineers looked at the accommodations in the Condor to assess where improvements could be made. C.R. himself recommended the spec for the entry door on the right-hand rear of the fuselage, effectively standardizing American's operations and keeping passengers out of the prop blast. (Pilots started the left engine first during normal operations.)

Perhaps the only aspect of the development that wasn't conducted with a benevolent spirit of cooperation was the competition for the engine contract. Both Curtiss-Wright and Pratt & Whitney made bids on the airplane, with each company hosting a team of engineers and production workers divided by an eight-foot wall in the Douglas plant. In the end, both secured a place in DC-3 history, with the original airplane delivered with the Wright R-1820 Cyclone 9 engines (1,000-hp each), and later models with the Pratt & Whitney 1830-series Twin Wasp engines (1,200-hp each) in several variants.

All told, more than 400 engineers worked on the program over the course of a just a few months in order to make it come together, and more than 3,500 drawings went into the DST's design.

Jackson McGowen was hired by Douglas Aircraft Company as a weight-and-balance engineer in 1939. "I was in the Engineering Weight group, led by a White Russian who escaped after the bad guys took over [in Russia]. I remember [Raymond] telling me that [original calculations I'd made] wouldn't work—I had to get every part of the wing in there in order to calculate the [moment of inertia]." He worked indirectly for Raymond—as Raymond was head of engineering by this time. "I might have told you the story of how Raymond made me stand for 15 minutes in his office while he read

$335.50

**Donald Douglas (middle)
and C.R. Smith (right)
in later years.**
*(Courtesy of Boeing
Douglas Archives)*

[something] before talking with me. [He was] prim, strong, with a sense of…oh, he was one of those people who could berate you with a smile. Later we took a trip through Europe together, then we were like family."

As for C.R. Smith, McGowen recalled, "[he was] one of the strongest men I met. Tough, a good administrator. I respected him even though he took me apart: 'Why did you do this or that?'"

1. Actual price of the phone call (in this chapter's title) referenced in: "Classic American Airlines," by Geza Szurovy
2. "The Legacy of the DC-3"
3. dc3history.org, Henry Holden/Allen Campbell
All quotes from Jackson McGowen are from the author interview.

Just Another Flight

Her polished props shone in the sun. They'd rolled her off the line just three days before, and all the standard preflight checks had been made. Everything about this airplane said economy—do it quickly—as the legions of engineers on both sides of the house had buckled down to complete the job. Getting it flown before Christmas would be a morale booster to be sure.

The clock struck 3 p.m., and Carl Cover and Frank Collbohm walked out the airplane. They'd done another test flight that morning, a DC-2 now being prepped for delivery. The black registration number "X14988" stood out on the tail. Fred Steinman was already on board.

Each man went about the task at hand, with callouts to each other that neither one would even remember saying out loud. The Douglas plant had manufactured hundreds of airplanes, and these men knew their jobs so well. It was routine.

After a 5-minute sit to let the engines warm up at the end of the runway, Cover once again commanded an airplane into history. The tension and the drama of the DC-1's first flight didn't even register in his mind, as he noted the liftoff within 1,000 feet. Performing according to the data.

After about an hour and a half, the airplane again touched ground and they taxied back to the ramp in front of Douglas. Cover shut down the engines. As the prop turned he caught a glimpse of the light off the silver propeller hub as the sun lowered in the sky.

4:30 p.m., December 17, 1935.

The airplane remembers the day even if her pilots do not.

IT WAS A QUIET DAY WHEN the DST first flew. Though little press went out prior to the DC-1's first flight, at least it was a big event around the factory. First flights back in the 1920s had involved pushing the airplanes out of the factory on Wilshire Boulevard, then down the road to Clover Field.

But on this sunny but cool day, not even company execs took time out to watch the flight—it wasn't even timed to the company lunch break. So only a few engineers and other workers witnessed the event.

Copyright© Boeing

Clover Field plant *(Courtesy of Boeing Douglas Archives)*

For Christmas 1935, Douglas' colleagues presented him with the original $25 hand drill that was the first piece of machinery owned by the Davis–Douglas Company back in 1920, responsible for helping the young company build *The Cloudster*.[1]

The first customer, American Airlines, accepted the first airplane in April 1936, after 25 hours and 41 minutes of test flight over the course of several months. The DST prototype, now designated NC14988, would become the *Flagship Texas*, but it only flew with American for a very short time before being sold to TWA in July 1936.

Walt Braznell captained the *Flagship Illinois* on American's inaugural DST flight, from Chicago to Newark, departing at noon

American Airlines *Flagship Texas*
(Courtesy of Boeing Douglas Archives)

Walt Braznell *(Courtesy of C.R. Smith Museum)*

on June 26, 1936.[2] Two other bases, New York and Newark, put DSTs into service at this time, beginning American's Flagship Service (though overnight flights—the true "sleeper" service—wouldn't begin until September). Braznell had begun his career as an airmail pilot, joining American precursor Robertson Airways in 1928. He had checked out in the DC-2 in May 1934, and he would be promoted to chief pilot for American Airlines' Chicago base in January 1937.

By the end of 1937, American had turned a profit, and was on its way to surpassing United and TWA as the leading passenger airline in the United States, in both revenue and passenger miles. Credit goes squarely to the DST and DC-3 for being the tool that made this possible.

---

1. Wilbur H. Morrison
2. "An Airman's Odyssey," by William Braznell

On the crisp February morning, the classroom felt like a chiller tacked on to the hangar, like a cinder-block afterthought, with none of the trappings of the stately Chicago Municipal Airport terminal building to the south—just a few rows of hard wood student desks that most of the boys coming in thought they'd left behind in high school. The carcass of an old Stinson huddled in the back, alongside a box-like contraption on rails, AA wings on the tail of it, one of the Link trainers. A couple of fellows had already taken up residence in the second and third rows, already wearing a uniform of a kind—suit jacket, tie, starched white shirt. Kelly straightened his jacket over his slight frame and captured a place for himself where he thought he'd be out of the line of fire.

Back out in Burbank, all his flying had been contact flying—navigating by landmarks and using a compass heading only on trips that took him away from the familiar territory of the L.A. Basin. The June gloom kept them grounded—or some intrepid souls broke up through it, and perhaps concocted an approach of sorts to get them back down. That's what the stubby-winged soap-box derby car behind him was for, he thought.

Spot on 8 a.m., a humorless man opened the door and made his way to the blackboard like an assemblage of mismatched parts, the survivor of a crack-up just a few years earlier that no one thought he'd live through. He surveyed the troops.

"Surely you were judiciously and assiduously bent over your route planning assignment last night until the far side of the clock, not playing poker for stamps on your sad little cots in the dorm. Keep your flight computers tucked safely away"—Kelly fingered the cardboard wheel under the flap of his jacket pocket—"and let's see who has met the mark." His sharp blue eyes penetrated the thick cloud of psychic cover that every young man in the room sought to shelter himself within.

A second instructor, McIntosh, chuckled from his seat at the Link. Kelly couldn't help but hum *sotto voce* (in a healthy bass that belied his size and 24 years) the opening bars of a song he'd danced to with that fine young lady over the holidays. "...it seems we stood and talked like this before...but I can't remember where or when..." Now, if only he could remember the assignment. Right, Buffalo to Newark.

A couple of chairs away, Chuck Sisto raised his hand. "Mr. Lester, I had a question about the assignment. You gave us a fuel load of 150 gallons a side in the mains and none in the aux tanks, and we're supposed to go from Buffalo to Newark with stops at Rochester and Syracuse and not take on any more? I could do it, but I'm not sure these other characters could without ending up on vapors."

William Lester turned his ragged face to assess young Sisto, another California cowboy bent on trying his patience. "Mr. Sisto, the point of the flight planning exercise is to develop critical thinking in your feeble minds. Situations will arise out there on the line that will require you to actually engage in multiplication and division at the request of your captain. And you had better be right. And you had better learn quickly when to radio ahead to the next stop for fuel because you idled a little too long in Albany."

"Now, Mr. Owen," addressing him now, but with an eye on Sisto, "Clearly your fellow Californian compatriot believes he is superior to the question—did you manage to make it from Buffalo to Newark?"

WILLIE LESTER'S COLLEGE OF KNOWLEDGE, the new-hires called it. "[William] Lester was a pilot on American that had cracked an airplane up," recalls Kelly Owen, a pilot who hired on with American Airlines in 1939. "He never did fly after that crash, but he still worked for American and he operated an instrument training school and checkout school." American referred to it as Copilot School, intended to quickly train the large number of new pilots the company was bringing in to fly the newest members of its Douglas fleet.

As head of the school, Lester was in charge of the six-week intensive ground school, teaching aerodynamics, meteorology, and navigation, among other topics. Colin McIntosh commanded the

Link Simulator
(Courtesy of C.R. Smith
Museum and American
Airlines, Inc.)

Link trainer—the early flight simulation device that resembled a child's toy made from a cardboard box more than it did an airplane. It was generally regarded as a means of torture for pilots, especially the claustrophobic. The mock airplane was outfitted inside with a cockpit and flight controls that physically moved the trainer and translated through the device into simulated movement across a representative map. An instructor sat at this map at a station outside the trainer and input conditions to test the unlucky fellow inside, such as simulated wind and turbulence.

Once inside, the pilot was closed off from outside references (the classroom) and had to successfully manipulate the controls in order to track the required courses set by the instructor. While not exactly fun for most trainees, it did serve the purpose of allowing pilots to practice flying solely by reference to the instrument panel without using more costly aircraft time or exposing themselves to the hazards presented by simulating certain emergencies in flight.

Most pilots were more than thankful to graduate and get on to real flying. Kelly Owen remembers: "[I hired on with American in] March 1939. First flight with them was in May 1939, in a DC-2. When we first were transferred from Chicago and completed first officer school in Chicago, we were sent to different bases, and Ernie Gann and a fellow by the name of Peterson and I were sent to Newark with Preston Mood…and George McCabe was the chief pilot and Tommy Boyd was the assistant. They took us out to give us three takeoffs and landings in the DC-2 [NC-14922] and three in a DC-3 [NC-17333] the same day to qualify us so we could fly the "Sun" schedule. Ernie, Preston and myself were all given our three takeoffs and landings in both airplanes.

"Then I was scheduled with Sam Ross to go from Newark to Syracuse to Rochester, Buffalo, Erie and Cleveland on my first trip [NC-14923, Flight No. 62, Air Mail Route 21], and we laid over in Cleveland and we came back the same way the following day. That was my first flight with American in the DC-2. And later on, the same month, I flew the DC-3. Of course, there was a big difference in the airplanes. There were controllable pitch [propellers] on the DC-2 but constant speeds on the DC-3, and I'll never forget how embarrassed I was. On the DC-2s, you just shift like a propeller control, suddenly, all at once, both sets. It would switch from high to low.

"Well, I took off from Newark with Ray Wonsey on the DC-3 [NC-16015, Flight No. 15, Air Mail Route 7] going to Chicago on a nonstop, and he let me climb out and level off at cruise. I got up to cruise, and I got the prop controls and pulled 'em back and they were the constant speeds on the DC-3, and, of course, the rpm just really came down and you could really hear it in the cabin too. Ray realized that I'd been flying the -2s and…that from habit I had just grabbed them and pulled them back, but it was a bit embarrassing. Passengers all thought the engines quit."

Every pilot who flew the line in the early days has a story about a particularly dictatorial captain with whom they were paired, and, by and large, the copilot was expected to quietly soak up the knowledge needed to eventually transition to the left seat. Sent onto paying flights with only a few landings in type, the green first officers would have a wide variety of flying backgrounds but only a small amount of specialized aircraft knowledge. Some captains warmed up to the role of teacher, but others never did, and their first officers learned by osmosis.

The captain would determine when the copilot would get a landing, too, and often copilots would go quite some time without one, depending on with whom they flew. Today, airlines have specific procedures for ensuring that both crew members get a chance to act as the flying pilot, but that wasn't the case when the DC-3 dominated the line.

However, the DC-3 was set up such that many items on the checklist could not easily be accomplished by the fellow in the left seat—the cockpit was clearly intended to be a two-man operation. The hydraulic system favors the right side of the cockpit, with the levers for operating the landing gear and flaps located below and just to the rear of the right seat. The long wobble pump handle is also more readily actuated from this side. And while not critical to flight yet still important to long engine life, the cowl flap actuators rise up on stems like a pair of aluminum tulips just to the right of the copilot on the sidewall. It is possible to "solo" a DC-3, but certainly captains availed themselves of the young man in the right seat for most of the heavy chores.

All quotes from Kelly Owen are from the author interview.

Flag Stop

Flying with a new captain—someone he hadn't flown with before—always set him a little bit on edge. You never knew what to expect with a new guy. But he'd been instructed to pick up the dispatch from the office on his way out to the airplane, so he said hello to the pretty girl behind the counter and took the paper in hand. The weather map on the wall showed stations out west reporting colder temperatures and some rain, headed their way in the next couple of days. But for now, fair skies for most of the day's work ahead.

Airmail Route 21 today. Albany, Syracuse, Rochester, Buffalo, Erie, Cleveland. Sometimes a layover in Buffalo and fly a trip to Toronto, but not by the way the paper in his hand read. The weather, being fair with light winds, made it possible they'd get the stop at Wilkes-Barre too, before heading on to Albany.

The late September day was fresh and cool, with a taste on the breeze marking that summer had passed. They may need that heater once airborne, if they got high enough. Not likely on these short legs. Maybe they wouldn't get up above 2,000 until they got over the hills, then maybe 4,000. Just a waste of gas to go any higher, especially if there was wind up there—probably, with that light breeze down here.

He grabbed a stack of fresh flight reports from the cubby, and headed out to the airplane for its preflight inspection. Mostly he needed to make sure the pins were out of the gear, as this was the first flight of the day and the *Flagship Pennsylvania* had been parked overnight.

A short while later, the captain boarded and turned to him briefly. "Brooke." From that, it sure felt like he'd be reduced to raising the pennant after landing, and that's about it. Seven years of flying, and who knows how many hours, for this? But he slid open the window to get some air on his face, and he cooled off quickly. There was something about sitting up on the perch, eighteen feet up in the air, that imbued him with pride beyond any flak he might suffer from the left seat. He'd be there some day.

The captain taxied them out to the newly-poured concrete at New York Municipal Airport—La Guardia Field. Smooth. Just cinders some places, with a concrete pad for run-up. And at Erie, they landed between the asphalt strips right in the grass, as the DC-3's gear stance was a little too wide for the narrow lines of pavement. Brooke lined them up on Runway No. 2, headed just east of due north to agree in part with the wind, and pushed forward the throttles to launch them toward upstate New York. With a head nod to him, he ordered the gear up, and the younger man complied.

The flagship pointed towards Syracuse. But a check with the last flight through eastern Pennsylvania confirmed the winds stayed light. Brooke steered toward Wilkes-Barre.

A few minutes later, the town settled out along the horizon just past the hills. A few more minutes, and they crossed over the airport. Turning abeam the runway to fly its length parallel, he asked him, "Do you see the flag out, son?"

He squinted into the sun to see the makeshift tower on the ground. He could just barely make out the man hoisting the yard of fabric into the air. "Sure do, sir." The captain reduced the throttles and settled onto downwind just past the Susquehanna River, commanding flaps and gear from his charge. He lined them up for the field, with the terrain coming into relief as they descended, and as they slipped in over the trees the breeze freshened a bit. A three-point touchdown in the Wyoming Valley grass. He rolled out just past the row of buildings.

The station manager came jogging out towards the airplane as Brooke turned it in a slow circle, avoiding what looked to be a soft spot where the grass got tall. A portly middle-aged man in a plaster-colored suit came out behind him, carrying a traveling kit and a birdcage. Brooke turned to him. "We stopped for this?" A sigh. "Guess it's all revenue."

～

AMERICAN AIRLINES INTRODUCED THE DC-3 SERIES into its system first with the Douglas Sleeper Transports (DSTs) that crossed the country in segments, with an average westbound flight time of about 15 hours. The DC-3 came on line in 1936, and quickly took over the majority of the route system, with most passengers along for shorter hops. The company kept DC-2s on its flight lines until around 1940, when it divested the last ones to Delta Airlines.

Compared to other commercial passenger aircraft of its time, such as the Boeing 247 and the Curtiss Condor—even its brother the DC-2—the DC-3 was a vast improvement for air travel for both passengers and pilots. Pilots liked the DST and DC-3 better because of improvements to the braking and hydraulic systems, as well as the more powerful engines (including the G-2, G-102 and 102A, and the Pratt & Whitney 1830–92), constant speed props (which were full feathering—another boon to safety), and better heating systems.

Yet traveling in the DC-3 was significantly different in many ways from air travel later in the 20th century. For example, the flights stayed low-level compared to those using modern jet aircraft. While state-of-the-art in the late 1930s, the DC-3 didn't have the pressurization or the environmental systems to make the cabin comfortable at higher altitudes (let alone the safety afforded by weather penetration equipment such as radar and modern anti-ice and deice systems—though the DC-3 had pneumatic deicing boots on the leading edges of its wings, and deicing fluid delivered to its props and windshield).

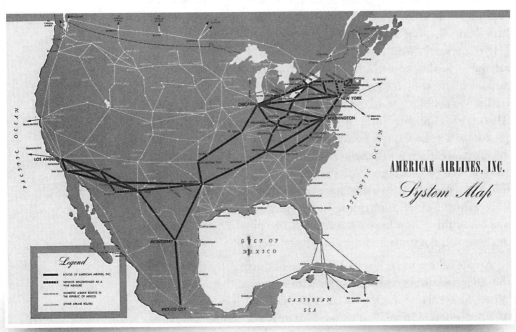

American Airlines route map, 1942 *(Courtesy of American Airlines, Inc.)*

Instead, the DC-3 excelled at shorter missions, with towns strung like pearls along each airline's route maps. Its capability to land in confined areas, carry up to 21 people (in standard daytime passenger configurations) and baggage, and fly safely through much of the weather proved its worth over and over.

Kelly Owen describes some of the early trips along these short-haul routes, and the flexibility—and sense of competition—in the crews. "You know some flights landed at Wilkes–Barre. A flag stop—if they had passengers they'd put out a flag, and you'd see it and land and pick them up. If they didn't have passengers you'd just pass 'em up and go on to Syracuse. They had a pretty heavy wind restriction there. If it was over a certain wind velocity, and directions weren't right, you weren't supposed to land. And of course we wanted to get all of the passenger revenue we could, and the station manager was anxious to have you land and pick up somebody, so we'd stretch that point on wind a lot, and this is where I got shot down two or three times.

Kelly Owen

"I'd be approaching either from the east or west and [another captain, Chuck Sisto, would have] just been there... [so I'd] ask him, 'Chuck, what kind of wind did you have at Wilkes–Barre?' [He'd answer,] 'Well it wasn't exactly within limits, but I landed anyway.' He shot you down, 'cause if you'd go in there and have any problem, they have it on record on [the wind] being out of limits. We'd risk it, but I had him pull it on me one time out of Albany, with the chief pilot riding on the jump seat out of Chicago. [I] took off at La Guardia and [was] going into Albany, and it was marginal weather, and Sisto was eastbound and I was westbound. He had just pulled out of Albany when I called in range, and he told me, 'Well, it was below limits but we made it.' And here we were with the chief pilot riding in the jump seat, and he told us it was below limits and here I was fixing to go in and land. I sneaked in there and got in there all right, but I never will forget that guy."

Airports, too, were still in development during this period, and the DC-3 adapted readily to the wide-ranging field conditions. When New York Municipal—La Guardia Field (later La Guardia Airport) opened in 1939, it showed many improvements—not the least of which was having several paved runways. This was not the case around the system, as Owen recalls.

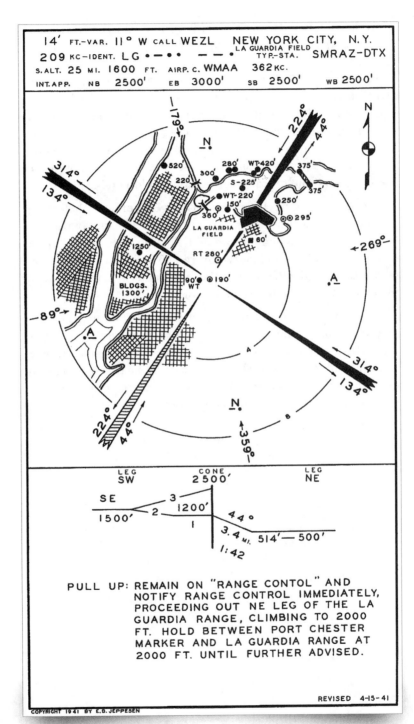

New York La Guardia in 1941 *(Courtesy of Jeppesen)*

"Boston was a cinder airport for a long time; it just had these concrete pads where we would run up, to protect the props on run-up when you're static. Syracuse had paved runways, and Rochester. The interesting thing about Rochester was it had a control tower that looked like it was just on one pipe, looked like a birdcage on top. [There] weren't too many airplanes that had radios, and some didn't have transmitters, just had receivers. At Rochester, [it was] not too unusual to hear them call a Cub or something taxiing out: 'If you read the tower, shake your ailerons.' The guy moved the ailerons to indicate he was receiving, but couldn't talk."

"I had a copilot by the name of George Kopf, and [before he was hired by American] he was flying for a newspaper outfit that had an autogyro." When they would fly into Rochester, "he'd pick up the mike and call and say, 'American 65 to Rochester, say if you read this, shake the tower.' And the guy would come out and rock the tower. We used to have a lot of fun."

Commercial passenger aircraft still had a long way to go before they would be optimized for flying across the country and over oceans. And when World War II started, the aircraft and crew were more valuable for use elsewhere, and services such as the flag stop were discontinued. But the DC-3 made these trips possible and reliable in a way they had not been before.

All quotes from Kelly Owen are from the author interview.

Golf Shoes

The Memphis night was already coming on, dusk falling down on the ramp when Walt came striding up to the airplane. He tucked his pipe absentmindedly in his pocket and grinned at the stewardess standing at the door.

"How's your game, Walt?" The young first officer called out from under the wing.

"Ah, couldn't stay out of the rough today...no luck...windy out there, you know," he replied. He shot his cuffs from under his jacket. Though the airline had uniform shirts, he preferred his own that he had hand-made. Had a whole rack of them, practically, left over from his dandy days on the show circuit, French cuffs and smooth cotton. He strolled over to the young man loading bags into the tail of the airplane. Dirty blue, scuffed leather, one tied with two wraps of twine, one that shone with polished brass; the luggage made neat rows on the cart before the man disappeared with them into the rear compartment.

"We full back there, yet?"

"No, sir, not yet." The man grinned. "Won't likely be on the sleeper, sir. Plenty of room for more bags."

"Good news, good news. Been hot out here these last days."

"Yes, sir." The man leaned over to grab another duffel. "Nice to be on the evening shift."

The first officer came around the wing and headed for the door. He shook his head at the captain, and continued on up the air stair. Walt breezed on up into the airplane behind him, and shook hands with each male passenger, with a nod to the ladies, as he waltzed up the aisle, the berths still tucked up behind panels overhead. He took his seat in the cockpit.

Let's get this off the ground, he thought. I've got another golf game tomorrow.

In the air, he could feel the little tick marks engraved in the trim wheel as he rolled it under his hand, seeking out that place where the DC-3 would ride as true as her claim. He hankered for one of the doughnuts a stewardess had just brought over from a trip to Winston–Salem...was it the doughnut, or was it the girl? He mused for a couple of minutes as the night settled around them. In the back, he knew that the stewardess was getting the booths ready, as the motion of her footsteps up and down the aisle rocked the airplane a little nose to tail. Such a little thing, but even so, when she stepped aft of the CG, everyone knew it.

Passengers climbed into the berths, drawing the curtains for a modicum of privacy, and tucking a white cotton sheet and gray wool blanket up around them. A light rain started against the glass in front of him. Dang, hope that doesn't turn into a real rain. This could be a long, wet night!

And here he was, still wearing his golf shoes.

Kelly Owen recalled the same gripe, which improved somewhat from the DC-2 to the DC-3, but didn't completely go away. "With each position report, we'd give weather, and it wasn't uncommon to hear a guy say, 'Overcast and light rain outside and heavy rain inside.' Those DC-2s leaked so bad that we had slicker-type capes that we'd put over our laps to keep them dry. That windshield would leak in just light rain and come through there. The DC-3 was much better in that respect, and they were even better once American put the bird deflectors on. You wouldn't get nearly the water [inside the cockpit that] you did before."

Of course, the bird deflectors were there for a reason. Owen

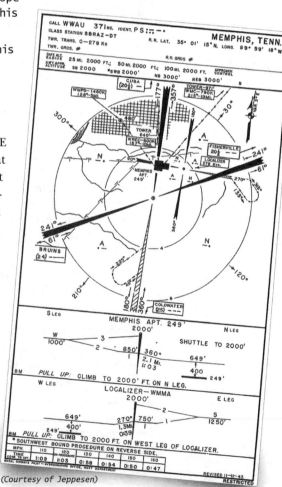

(Courtesy of Jeppesen)

TOGETHER WE *Fly* VOICES FROM THE DC-3

said, "We had some mud hens penetrate the windshield on a DC-3 going into Knoxville—it hit the copilot's windshield, but it came through diagonally and hit the bulkhead right behind the captain. And put a big whomp in there and that bulkhead had a fire ax on it and it hit that and it still bent it. Just a mud hen, [with the airplane] at approach speed. So American put what they called a 'duck deflector' or a bird deflector in the 'V' part of the windshield, and it would change the airstream; it altered the flow pattern."

The sleeper service was reasonably popular, with the DST version of the airplane carrying 12 passengers for the overnight, long-haul service. But flying coast to coast on the DC-3 still meant an average of 12 hours eastbound, and up to 18 hours westbound, because of

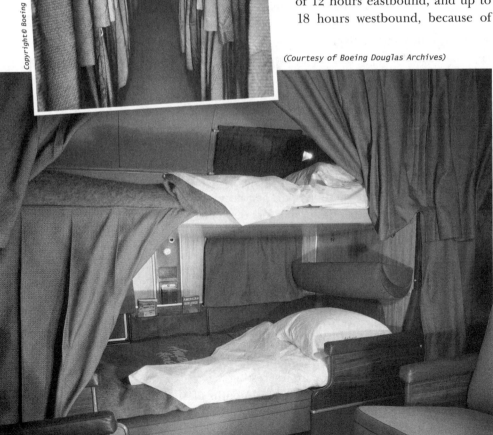

(Courtesy of Boeing Douglas Archives)

greater prevailing headwinds on the westbound tracks. Sleeper service cost an extra $3 to $8 one way, depending on the trip length, on top of fares up to $270 round trip for a flight from New York to Los Angeles. A full-course dinner and a hot breakfast were part of the fare—the DST was the first commercial airplane in the United States with the kitchen facilities to serve hot food.

While the cabin service made great strides forward, the path for a copilot to upgrade to captain was still not well-defined, with little formal training. So some captains took it upon themselves to ensure that the copilots they flew with got the opportunity to practice being pilot-in-command under the supervision of a senior man before going out on the line on their own. "We used to do this illegally, against the company rules," Owen said, "but [captains] would put us over there [in the left seat]. I had a nice group of captains I flew with and put me in the left seat all the time and let me fly—hell, they'd doze off!"

"And [when I made captain], I was doing that with my crew, and I had a station manager at Syracuse who didn't like me worth a damn, and he decided he was going to screw me up. [He] said I arrived on such and such a flight on such and such a date and the copilot was in the captain's seat. And when the chief pilot got the report, he asked, 'Is this true?' and I said. 'Yeah, this is true." He said, "You know we have a regulation against that." I said, "There isn't any regulation against me flying from the right." And I had 'em there. I said, "How does that station manager know I wasn't flying that airplane from the right? He can't prove the copilot was flying from the left, and there isn't any regulation that says I can't fly it from the right." Now, pilots go through specific transition courses when they make the first upgrade to captain, and they fly their first trips as captain with passengers on board typically under the supervision of a line check airman or chief pilot.

Radiator Cap Girl

Zoe Dell Lantis snatched up the opportunity to work as an "exposition girl" at the Golden Gate International Exposition in San Francisco in 1939. Referred to as San Francisco's "world's fair," the exposition celebrated the opening of the Golden Gate Bridge just six months prior. Lantis (now Zoe Dell Nutter) was a dancer just 20 years old and looking for an interesting way to expand her horizons. And she did just that—and for months after the show closed—when she was offered the job to criss-cross the country on an aerial promotional tour.

Commercial air travel was in its early, rambunctious childhood, still suffering unduly from scrapes and scrapping amongst the regulators. But the promotion of air travel hit its stride in the late 30s, and in an early marketing tie-in that would make modern swains proud, Zoe Dell was hired to fly around the country delivering invitations to San Francisco's party in United DC-3s.

The airlines in the late 1930s were keen to sell the safety and comfort of their new Douglas DC-3s, so United leveraged the Golden Gate exposition (which featured modern modes of transportation among its many, many exhibits) to feature the airplane around the United States. The tour took the crews along with exposition girls like Zoe Dell back and forth for weeks. Zoe Dell figured that she logged as many miles during those weeks as anyone who wasn't a pilot. The airlines featured the girls with the concept that if a young woman wasn't afraid to fly, then a mature businessman shouldn't be either.

Courtesy of Zoe Dell Nutter

Zoe Dell donned the cute little outfit that kitted her in silver with a smirk—she would be a "radiator cap girl"! Whatever did that mean? She guessed that she just looked like one—a cap, that is. She launched service with the smack of a champagne bottle on the hulls of several DC-3s during her tenure.

Whatever the actual influence these "radiator cap girls" had on ticket sales is unknown—but the experience certainly left its mark

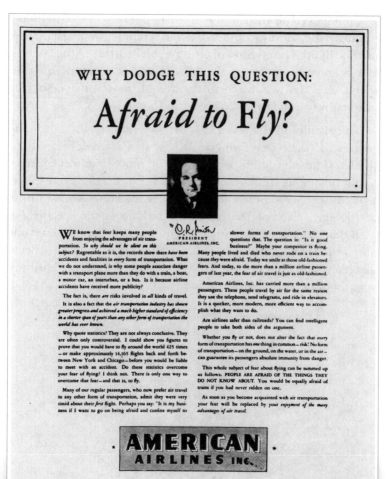

The text inside the advertisement reads:

WHY DODGE THIS QUESTION:

Afraid to Fly?

WE know that fear keeps many people from enjoying the advantages of air transportation. *So why should we be silent on this subject?* Regrettable as it is, the records show there *have been* accidents and fatalities in *every* form of transportation. What we do not understand, is why some people associate danger with a transport plane more than they do with a train, a boat, a motor car, an interurban, or a bus. Is it because airline accidents have received more publicity?

The fact is, there *are* risks involved in *all* kinds of travel. It is also a fact that the *air transportation industry has shown greater progress and achieved a much higher standard of efficiency in a shorter span of years than any other form of transportation the world has ever known.*

Why quote statistics? They are not always conclusive. They are often only controversial. I could show you figures to prove that you would have to fly around the world 425 times — or make approximately 14,165 flights back and forth between New York and Chicago — before you would be liable to meet with an accident. Do these statistics overcome your fear of flying? I think not. There is only one way to overcome that fear—and that is, to fly.

Many of our regular passengers, who now prefer air travel to any other form of transportation, admit they were very timid about their *first* flight. Perhaps you say: "It is my business if I want to go on being afraid and confine myself to slower forms of transportation." No one questions that. The question is: "Is it good business?" Maybe your competitor is flying. Many people lived and died who never rode on a train because they were afraid. Today we smile at those old-fashioned fears. And today, to the more than a million airline passengers of last year, the fear of air travel is just as old-fashioned.

American Airlines, Inc. has carried more than a million passengers. These people travel by air for the same reason they use the telephone, send telegrams, and ride in elevators. It is a quicker, more modern, more efficient way to accomplish what they want to do.

Are airlines safer than railroads? You can find intelligent people to take both sides of the argument.

Whether you fly or not, does not alter the fact that *every* form of transportation has *one* thing in common—risk! No form of transportation—on the ground, on the water, or in the air—can guarantee its passengers absolute immunity from danger.

This whole subject of fear about flying can be summed up as follows: PEOPLE ARE AFRAID OF THE THINGS THEY DO NOT KNOW ABOUT. You would be equally afraid of trains if you had never ridden on one.

As soon as you become acquainted with air transportation your fear will be replaced by your *enjoyment of the many advantages of air travel.*

C. R. Smith
PRESIDENT
AMERICAN AIRLINES, INC.

AMERICAN AIRLINES INC.

American Airlines ad featuring C.R. Smith
(Courtesy of C.R. Smith Museum and American Airlines, Inc.)

on Zoe Dell, who learned to fly and worked throughout her life in the aviation industry.

It was about this same time that American Airlines came out with its famous ad, "Afraid To Fly?" featuring American Airlines president C.R. Smith. Though it was hard to determine if these campaigns to assuage the general public's concerns about aviation safety proved effective, they certainly were memorable. The truth? The growing statistics demonstrating fewer accidents in spite of vastly increased flight miles flown following the introduction of the DC-3 was the best advertising of all.

All quotes from Kelly Owen are from the author interview.
All quotes from Zoe Dell Nutter are from the author interview.

There was a commotion outside the window, coming from just down the street, and Kip ran to the open pane to catch a better look. He leaned out and the stagnant air wrapped his face with its damp fingers. It was hard to see into the dark night, even without the mist, with no moon to light up the street.

A truck toiling under a heavy load came out of the darkness, grinding over the cobblestones. A man shouted, "A little more right! More right!" to an unseen partner. Kip tried to puzzle what it was that the truck strained to tow, and he stretched a little further out the window to see the happenings from his second-floor perch. The cobblestones were slick beneath the truck's tires, and every so often one slipped over a glossy bump, losing traction then gaining it back in the rut between the stones.

Finally, a shadowy figure loomed through the soft dark air, and Kip rubbed his eye to try and resolve what he saw—whatever it was, it was huge! Filling the street and the top of it at his eye level. The shape was almost like a ship's prow, in the middle, but then he saw this prow was flanked by two round nacelles. Could it be? An airplane? Sure enough, it came rolling past on gigantic tires that looked like they would dwarf him should he be standing in the street below.

Across the way he saw Mrs. Vandermullen lean out and cry as she too reconciled the thing moving past with the dream from which she'd just awakened. This airplane, she thought, its wings clipped from its passage on the deck of some container ship from America, across from the states to her little village on the outskirts of Antwerp. Now rolling down her street, from the port to the *luchthaven*, a mile away. All that effort, for what, she wondered.

Would that airplane—or one of its sister ships—save her life, and that of the boy across the street? She didn't know, just shook her head and went back to bed. But in just a few years' time, that awful VH-1 buzz bomb would take away every last thing standing in her village, and yes, perhaps that airplane she saw pushing its way from port to airport, would carry the loads that would keep her fed, and provide cover and a modicum of safety for Kip as he conscripted into the Second World War.

~

DOUGLAS RECOGNIZED THAT THE EUROPEAN MARKET was important to the expansion of the company. He had formed a friendship with Anthony (Tony) Fokker after the Dutch aircraft manufacturer became fond of the DC-1 after flying it during its development. Fokker had established an American arm of his company in 1923, the Atlantic Aircraft Corporation, and he based it in New York. Douglas granted Fokker the rights to the DC-2's European sales and manufacturing; it would follow that the company would be interested in the same role with the DC-3.

To most efficiently move aircraft from the United States to Europe—and to more completely ensure their successful crossing of the Atlantic Ocean—Fokker and Douglas arranged that the DC-3 would travel as deck cargo on container ships. The aircraft would arrive in port at Amsterdam, be moved to Fokker's Nederlandse Vliegtuigenfabriek (Dutch Aircraft Factory) plant, and reassembled and made ready for delivery.

Five of these aircraft reassembled at Amsterdam went to Swissair (Schweizerische Luftverkehr AG). The Swiss national airline, founded in March 1931, had developed its business flying the Fokker VII b and Lockheed Orion aircraft between major cities in Switzerland and throughout western Europe. Perhaps following a similar model to that of American, Swissair added a Curtiss Condor to its fleet in 1934. When Douglas introduced the DC-2, the airline had six of these assembled and delivered from Fokker, so it was only natural that when the larger, more advanced DC-3 came along, the

The jack point with "HB-IRO," c/n 2054.

company would see fit to add them to their fleet. The first two, HB-IRA (c/n 1945) and HB-IRI (c/n 1946), were delivered to Swissair in June 1937.

Douglas produced all of its aircraft using a "construction number," which gave the aircraft's placement overall in the manufacturing scheme. Wanting to set a precedent that he was an established manufacturer, the first Douglas aircraft, *The Cloudster*, was Construction Number 100 ("c/n 100"). Gaps in the numbering denote lots set aside by Douglas and not used. The first of the DC-3 series, N14988, was Construction Number 1494, and production of the DC-3s was interspersed with DC-2s, B-18s, and observation aircraft.

Construction Number 2054, HB-IRO, came out of the Douglas factory in early October 1938, and was delivered on October 31. The aircraft had been test-flown in Santa Monica for its airworthiness certificate, and then flown to New York's Idlewild Airport for disassembly. It traveled the North Atlantic under a protective canvas covering on the deck. Though previous aircraft had come in through the ports of Rotterdam and Cherbourg, HB-IRO came into the port at Antwerp, Belgium, and was towed through the city

HB-IRO in Swissair livery *(Courtesy Douglas Aircraft, via Scott Thompson Collection)*

**Aircraft waiting
shipment to Europe**
*(Courtesy of Boeing
Douglas Archives)*

at night to the airport at Duerne for reassembly by Fokker mechanics, and test flight by Fokker pilots.

In Fall 1939, one more DC-3 was delivered as the airspace closed in Western Europe to civilian traffic. At the outset of World War II, the airport at Antwerp was bombed and significantly damaged by local engineering corps, but the German occupying troops repaired the damage and used it throughout the war.

Following World War II, Fokker shifted its mission to reconfigure military versions of the DC-3, primarily the C-47, into commercial service for resale to European airlines getting back to normal schedules. Swissair took delivery of 11 more of these repurposed C-47s, and kept them in service until it divested the aircraft in the mid-1950s and the early 1960s. All told, Fokker had reassembled and distributed 63 DC-3s prior to the war. It is unclear how many C-47s Fokker refurbished after the armistice, though at least another dozen appear to have gone directly into Dutch registration numbers following the war.

The young crew assembled on the flight deck. With but 20 hours of time in the airplane between them, the pair brought measures of fear, naïveté, and excitement on board in their packs.

The captain's brow barely touched the inner band of his cap, and it rode cockeyed on his head. He almost knocked it off bending to slip himself into the left seat.

The copilot—barely out of high school—too young to be anxious about the task ahead—dropped himself into the right seat while the load agent strapped into the jump seat behind them.

The 25-knot crosswind whistled past the buildings that lined the runway at Kansas City. The major said the airplane must be ferried that day, and that captain was so anxious to prove he was equal to the task, equal to the airplane that could fit a row of Cubs inside. He knew way more about Cubs, that was for certain.

The crew was behind the 8-ball even as they took the runway. In a burst of adrenaline the captain shoved the throttles to full power, on the ready-to-overhaul engines. The rush of running at METO overwhelmed him such that he let the airplane lift off in a three-point attitude: He didn't push on the yoke at all in the takeoff roll that barely stretched three sets of edge lights on the newly paved runway. The airplane clawed skyward, roaring.

Heat built quickly as the cooling air was stolen from the intakes by the steep climb, and before he could call for the gear they were over the far end of the runway clearing 700 feet above the ground. The copilot's hands were sweaty and he fumbled at the gear latch. Frustrated, he knew it was his job to bring that gear up and now, dammit, so he left the latch and grabbed the hydraulic lever. It sealed his fate—the gear was soon bound and the captain, so nervous he couldn't even snap at him, went heads down with him to try and reconcile the gear.

Mere minutes passed, and they were at 5,000 feet. By chance, the captain stole a glance at the engine gauges and the paralyzing cold crept over his back as he realized what he'd done. The CHTs on both engines were already screaming at the tops of the dials, and the oil pressure on the left had sunk low.

He sent the load agent back to look at the left one as the copilot finally reset the gear and it slid into place. The big tires rode up in the wells, and finally, finally, the captain pushed the nose over and reduced power on the struggling engines.

As the agent comes back into the gangway, with his old news that the cowl looked fine, the captain saw an awful sight out his side window: the prop stopped, frozen into place. He recognized then that he'd been holding the rudder pressure for an undeterminable time—his legs carried the tension in his body so acutely that he couldn't notice the load until the sight of the silver blade reflecting dully in the weak sun snapped him into focus.

Blade flat to the wind, oil pressure lost, he couldn't feather the prop and reduce the drag. The result of his folly—the 5,000 feet of altitude they'd gained—was now the only thing that could save him.

His mind raced ahead, remembering the problems that the copilot had raising the gear, and as he turned the craft back toward the airport now many miles away, he ordered the rapidly maturing copilot to put the gear down at once.

But as the mighty gear legs locked down over center, he realized again that his impulsivity, his panic had painted him into a corner. The right engine, his only friend in this mess, one that had already seen flagrant abuse just minutes ago—it had to come back to METO power.

And yet this wasn't enough to overcome the product of his mistakes: the stopped left prop, the gear hanging out into the slipstream. The drag on the airplane was immense, and it clenched his stomach all the way into the seat.

The copilot called to the tower—to the thin air, truly—that they needed the field open. A voice disjointed from the thick reality of the cockpit offered them any runway.

Later the captain would reflect in a ghostly voice that he was not sure how they made that blessed end of the runway, the precious altitude falling away with each second—they may as well have been a glider—and they would have to land with the drag of the one dead engine and its three paddles fighting full power on the other—back into that same crosswind in a 25,000-pound taildragger.

He never remembered the details of the landing, but he remembered all too well the sight of the metal-like tin foil in the oil sumps as the mechanics dropped the pans later that afternoon. That foil that once was his engines—the whole airplane could have been nothing but foil—with him and his crew balled up inside it.

In 1942, as the United States entered the war in full, it became clear that the Air Ferrying Command would need a broader scope, and it was thus renamed the Air Transport Command. With this change, the newly born "ATC" effectively centralized the strategic transportation needs of the armed forces. This allowed the ATC to coordinate with various commands yet remain independent of them.

WASP waving to a C-47 *(Courtesy of Boeing Douglas Archives)*

Kelly Owen recalls one change specifically meant to address the new realities of needing to train pilots in a short period of time, and send them out as inexperienced crews—not a new co-pilot under the supervision of a seasoned captain: "I never made wheel landings with the airplane until I got into the Troop Carrier [Group] in World War II. And the reason they were doing that was not by choice, it was because we had students who were coming out of single-engine school, and we were trying to teach them how to fly a twin-engine plane and tow a glider in 30 days' time.

"It was a lot easier to teach them to fly it right to the ground, and hold it there, and then pull the power off. You could set up on a rate-of-climb indicator a rate of descent of 600 to 800 feet per minute and just hold that and go right to the ground, and it would [make for] a smooth touchdown. And then you just close the throttles, drop the tail down and close the flaps. So it was a lot easier for them to learn that quick than it was for us to teach them 3-point [landings, which required a bit more finesse]."

As the country ramped up to enter World War II, and the DC-3 was pressed into military service, a large number of new transport pilots—many of whom had never seen anything bigger than a Cub—signed on for duty. The forgiving nature of the airplane, the redundancy and robustness of its systems, surely saved many greenhorns from themselves in the long years of the war.

Working the Line

Douglas started the morning by driving southeast. With no staff meeting to require him in the office first thing, he steered his car onto the highway. On the flats near the airport at Long Beach, the crew would soon be busy siting the new plant. He was conscientious about driving in view of the workers, when they didn't have the luxury of a late-model car with the war going on. But he wanted to go out there one more time before they started moving earth.

Space—it's all about having the space, he thought. The space and the room and the favorable zoning and permits and a good relationship with the city so you can go long when you need to—and draw back when the cycle is down.

He had lost it at Santa Monica years ago, almost at the point they started building the DC-3 they'd been hemmed in. Even with the war looming, that wouldn't change. They covered over buildings with net, fake trees, false fronts—still hemmed in. The town politicos didn't say it so expressly, yet, but he felt it. Even at El Segundo, in that curve of the road, he felt it. Limited. It was in his nature to stay conservative with expansion, though.

Down at Long Beach he saw the plot of land that could hold the next line—and a state-of-the-art building—a monster line. Enough line to turn out 10,000 airplanes. More. It would only make sense when the country went to war full scale, with everyone chipping in—for a while. But what the hell? The contract was in hand. Those fellows on the war board pushed him to it. They'd build at Chicago, and Oke City, and Tulsa too. We'll rise to it.

Fast forward just a couple of years.

There, in that new factory at Long Beach, the lunch break was nearly over, the whistle about to sound. Marie made her way back from the table crowded with the other gals from the floor. She tumbled the chit over and over in her hand without much thought to it. Her employee number at Douglas stamped on the face of it gave her the ability to exchange it for a part. She had ten of these, issued to her when she was hired on. She wished it was a golden coin to bring Charlie back home.

They'd given her three days' pay as she learned how to buck a rivet: place the rivet head in the gun, hold it steady against the sheet as her partner held the block, breathe, and pull the trigger. She smiled the first few...well, she wrecked more than that, letting the gun slip off the rivet head before she could pull back cleanly, but soon she got the hang of it. The C–47s they were working on used razor head rivets in her section of the line, and she felt them jingle in her apron as she walked back to her station.

Her partner, Josie, was already back from the break. "You think it could get any hotter in here?" Josie took off her blue bandana and wiped her cheeks and chin.

"At least they have the fans going. Not sure how we'd make it if those stopped turning!" The heat she could handle—she and Charlie had moved out to California from Oklahoma a couple of years ago looking for work. Now they had work in spades—he was somewhere in the Pacific, on an LST leaving Hawaii for the Philippines. And here she was, sweating out every ounce she took in riveting on the line at DAC. The gun, though, felt solid in her hand, and she knew the rhythm of the rivets driving into the aluminum skin would take her mind off of the lonely bed she'd be in tonight.

"I AM NOT A PROPHET OR a philosopher. I am only an engineer," said Douglas.[1] He understood that to be a good pilot and a good designer were two separate things—he never learned to fly himself, and he knew that his calling was in shepherding a design from inspiration through production. Plenty for a man to think about without concerns of staying current and proficient in the air.

Though he was generally shy and quiet, he was open and nearly affectionate with his longtime staff, going to shirtsleeves often and putting an arm around a colleague. He knew his employees, no matter their position, and paid attention to the details of their lives. As one longtime Douglas worker related, "Douglas had a reputation for being tight on wages and everything—you know, he was a Scotsman and all that. I found that this wasn't true, at least not by the time I was hired [in the late 1930s]. The pay scale was up with the industry."

Douglas loved the sea, and naval projects and amphibious designs were sprinkled through the Douglas production history. But more than anything, he loved being out on the water and at one point qualified for the Olympic sailing team. He won a silver medal in the 1933 Olympics in his six-meter boat, *Gallant.* He taught himself to play the bagpipes proficiently, and would serenade colleagues and friends while on the water.

Douglas (left) often played for friends on his sailboat, *Endymion.* *(Courtesy of Boeing Douglas Archives)*

He spoke with candor, directness, and honesty. He was considered kind, thoughtful, and a constructive critic. He believed in direct management, building relationships with the various teams within the company.

He eventually developed a morning ritual which consisted of rising at 7:30, having an egg, toast, and black coffee for breakfast, and then driving the 10 minutes to work at the Santa Monica office in his latest car (he often had a new one, courtesy of local dealers in exchange for advertising). He smoked a pipe, cigars, and unfiltered cigarettes, and was generally a man of routine.

Douglas was not easy with strangers, and his first wife, Charlotte, was the far more outgoing of the pair. He would abandon social

Donald Douglas at the Santa Monica plant. Behind him is a United Airlines Douglas Sleeper Transport. *(Courtesy of Boeing Douglas Archives)*

engagements at home in favor of going out on his boat, or staying at home in peace and quiet. He encouraged his sons to build models (James Douglas recalls fetching scraps of balsa wood from the model shop at the factory) and to test their designs fully. He gave them encouragement, but not entitlement.

Jackson McGowen, who retired from McDonnell–Douglas as president of Douglas Aircraft in 1973, had enormous respect for Douglas. "I admired him more that anyone else I ever met. He was courteous, but withdrawn." On his boat, McGowen recalled that Douglas was perhaps a little more gregarious but still of a piece. "One time I was on his yacht with him out to Catalina, and he got in the little boat to go fish. He got word that a phone call came in—FDR wanted to talk with him immediately. He said, 'I'll come when I can,' and 30 minutes later answered the call."

The Douglas Aircraft Company grew enormously following the debut of the DC-3. Dale Berkihiser had applied for a job as an engineer out of junior college in 1937, and when they couldn't hire him into that area, he sought additional skills as a welder. They called him back shortly, with an opening, though not in engineering. He

IT TAKES ALL THREE

FOR

VICTORY

GATE Nº 4

DC-3 plant gate at Santa Monica
(Courtesy of Boeing Douglas Archives)

recalled, "I went to the Douglas factory on Ocean Park Boulevard in Santa Monica, to the human resources office. The sign on the wall read something like, 'We are the largest aircraft company in the world, with 3,000 employees.' They offered me a job, asking would I learn how to rivet if 'we paid you while you were learning.'"

Berkihiser accepted the job on the day shift, which paid 40 cents an hour. After a short bout of training, he had sufficiently acquired the technique to go onto the production line, where he worked on B-18s and DC-3s, riveting and doing some welding as well. "The DC-3 sold for $125,000, minus the engines and avionics," said Berkihiser. "And I remember that the wingtip, which was four feet long, cost $1,100."

After six months on the line, Berkihiser moved over to tooling, where he spent five years. He eventually made it onto Douglas' engineering team, becoming a design engineer. By that time, he lived in Long Beach, and for a period traveled the 20 air miles from the Long Beach Airport (where the Douglas plant was dedicated in 1941) to Santa Monica in a DC-3 flown by Stewart Airlines. These DC-3s were painted a light green. "We called it 'The Green Hornet,'" said Berkihiser. "I came to love the way it flew, like a gliding gull." The DC-3 still flies regularly from Long Beach under the flag of Catalina Flying Boats, an air cargo operator that provides delivery service to Catalina Island, off the coast of California.

During World War II, as men went oversees to fight, women took their places on the production lines in factories across the

C-47 production line at Long Beach *(Courtesy of Boeing Douglas Archives)*

At Long Beach
*(Courtesy of Boeing
Douglas Archives)*

country. Douglas Aircraft was no different—and the ladies weren't just sewing the fabric onto control surfaces (the first real production-line job that women took in numbers). They bucked rivets and performed nearly all the jobs that the men would. The neat rivet lines you see on aircraft made during the war years attest to their skill.

Wartime production of the Douglas DC-3 in its military variants didn't come about in a slam-dunk. Jackson McGowen recalled, "The search for a military cargo aircraft started in 1932 with the DC-2; we ended up selling them the C-39—really a DC-3 tail with a DC-2 fuselage. "The committee on wartime production involved [Robert] Collier and Grover Loening [an aircraft manufacturer], and they didn't have any transports in the early 1940s, [so they were] looking at aircraft to produce. [Originally] the DC-3 was turned down because it was too small, too light, not modern enough…but [we knew] we could produce a heck of a lot of them in a short time."

The DC-3 was changed, in McGowen's estimation, about 20 percent in order to meet the needs of the armed forces, and the primary military version, the C-47, was born. "The changes were determined by negotiation with the Army Air Corps," McGowen said. "The process began while we were already building things for France and England, so when the U.S. government decided to go in, we were almost ready.

"Two [major] things: the interior—side benches, and the [reinforced] floors for cargo. And a major change: the government paid for fancy tooling—steel and iron—we had been using 2 by 4s, you know. [We] built one a day at Long Beach at the peak of production." Berkihiser also recalled this change. For a time, he worked in the fuselage department at Long Beach, and he recalled the steel jigs spanning two levels of the shop. The investment, enabled by wartime production, that Douglas made in its materials and tooling contributed to the company's long-term success. A total of 10,632 military versions of the DC-3/C-47 were built before the end of World War II in the factories at Santa Monica, Long Beach, and Oklahoma City.

1. Frank Cunningham

All quotes from James Douglas are from the author interview.
All quotes from Jackson McGowen are from the author interview.
All quotes from Dale Berkihiser are from the author interview.

A Low Moon

A low moon hung over the horizon off his wing as the C-53D bore through the night. The lieutenant had handed McDonald the dispatch bearing his orders earlier that evening with a frown. Always a first time—new crew, new captain. Him. He rubbed his jaw, feeling the straw-colored fuzz along the bone. Getting thinner on the sawdust sausages and rations he'd gladly trade for cardboard.

It had been a rush to get off. The crew now assigned to the airplane with him didn't have a rhythm yet, and they wasted time—daylight—getting their act together. He looked over at the even younger man sitting in the right seat. Jimmie.

He dropped the pencil he used to scratch down the fuel load and it vibrated along the cockpit floor. He flipped up the cockpit lights and rubbed his eyes again when they stung from the change from dark to less dark. Picking up the pencil by his left foot, he noticed the airspeed indicator, now glowing, over the horn of the yoke. Zero. Buried in the dial.

"Cripes." He tapped the gauge. No sign of life. He reached over to his copilot, and gestured at the left-side airspeed dial. "Mine's dead," he said to Jimmie through the crackle static in the headset.

He remembered the copilot's gauge, far over to the right, and he looked. Zero.

They looked at each other. What could it be? in the look they exchanged.

"Maybe it's some mud up in there," said Jimmie.

McDonald thought for a moment, and then shook his head. "No. Two tubes. One for the left, one for the right. What's the chance of them both being messed up?"

"Aw, right."

McDonald unbuckled his belt. "You got it for a minute." He climbed out of the seat, careful not to kick the gear and flap handles near the floor between them. The metal sleeve where they stored the covers and pins was in the narrow companionway. He stood for a moment before he got the courage to feel in there. He pulled out the gear pins, and an extra bungee for the aileron lock. No pitot tube covers. All of a sudden he missed those pieces of red leather like a girl back home.

His first night landing in the airplane. Ever. And he had to do it without a damned airspeed indication.

He buckled back into the lap belt and gave Jimmie the bad news. The boy paled even in the red glow of the panel lamps.

"Can't we do anything to shake 'em off, sir?"

He considered the idea. "Don't think so." Another moment of consideration passed, and then he lit up with his own. "Maybe I can burn 'em off with the pitot heat!"

"Yeah! Well...it's worth a shot!"

So he reached up to the overhead and flipped the two toggles that would send heat through the tubes. They were meant to clear out ice and snow. He saw the load on the voltmeter. And he waited.

Looked at one airspeed dial, then the other. And waited.

Nothing.

He thought of how the heat would make the tube hot enough to scald his hand raw if he touched it. But was it hot enough to burn? They pressed on.

A long hour later they came to the field at Detaine, halfway to Nancy. He called the tower at the small field.

"—you're cleared to land. No other traffic at the field." The front end of the transmission was garbled but he shrugged it off.

"Roger that, cleared to land." He throttled back and held the nose up as he felt the air noise lessen. He guessed. "Quarter flaps." Jimmie complied.

Less air noise. The lights around the runway grew from pin dots to Christmas lights. "Half flaps." The lever went down again. "Gear."

Jimmie lowered the red lever, waited for the drag, and then popped the gear latch handle into place. "Down and latched, handle neutral, pressure's up, green light," he called.

The speed bled off. He felt it. Was he right? It felt okay, but all his outside references were essentially gone. All he had were the lines of light, and a bunch of men needing his cargo on the ground. And he surely didn't have the gas to loiter until dawn.

Half-mile final and the tower called. "Aircraft on final, wave off! Go around!"

McDonald jumped from his trance and looked at Jimmie. "Gear up!" He pushed the throttles forward. "Flaps up!"

"What was that?" asked Jimmie after he reset the handles.

"I don't know. But looks like we're doing it again." He carved around to the left in a wide arc through the night as the runway lights fell off below them.

They lined up again. This time he felt strangely more at ease. It seemed to work last time. Quarter flaps. Half. The progression standard. Only difference was no number on the dial to back up what he knew in his gut.

"Gear down, Jimmie. We're landing this time."

The next moment: "Aircraft in the pattern, cleared to land. We saw that you're a Gooney when you passed over us—thought you were the Black Widow coming in!"

McDonald chuckled. "Three-quarter flaps." It felt stable. The air was calm in the blackness. "Full."

They came over a group of shadows below—trees, fences—he'd find out in the morning. The touchdown was like sliding his arm straight into the satin-lined sleeve of his flight jacket, the big girl feeling for the planks as if with his fingertips.

"Hoorah!" Jimmie slapped his knee as the tail came down. The loadmaster and crew in back had no idea.

After rolling up to the line building, McDonald let Jimmie get out first. He could hear him as he ran to the front of the airplane.

"Aw, boss, you gotta see this!"

McDonald came down the stepladder and around to the nose. There in the spotlight he saw two red leather sleeves, warped into permanent fixture on the slim aluminum tubes.

JENE MCDONALD'S CREW GAINED RESPECT FOR him that night, in spite of the missed covers. He'd proven his skill, and his calmness under pressure. He was with the 31st, which was stationed out of AAF Station 519, in Grove, England. The 31st was there from 1943 to 1945; Jene was in Class 44E, which graduated in May 1944 from Advanced Pilot Training at Stockton, California. "The Navy wouldn't take me because of an overbite, but I had passed the air force tests. So I went through primary flight training for the Army Air Corps at Ryan Air Field in Tucson, and graduated from advanced flight school at Stockton Army Air Base in 1944. I went straight into the C-47 in the European theater."

He flew 50 hours in the C-47 to check out to the left seat. McDonald went over with friend Joe McCarten from Detroit, who also went into the Troop Carrier Group, but McCarten had to fly 200 hours in the right seat before he was checked out. McDonald was put on a train to the East Coast soon after, and then on a ship to England. That ship was a World War I-era German ship, the *King Edmund Alexander*, a beautiful cruise ship full of mahogany. He was 19, not yet 20, when he was assigned a crew on a C-53D.

The C-53D, a variant on the C-47, was configured strictly for troop carrier operations, particularly paratroopers. It had the small door on the right hand side of the fuselage, with seats inside, and handles for the paratroopers.

C-47s flying over Europe *(Courtesy of Boeing Douglas Archives)*

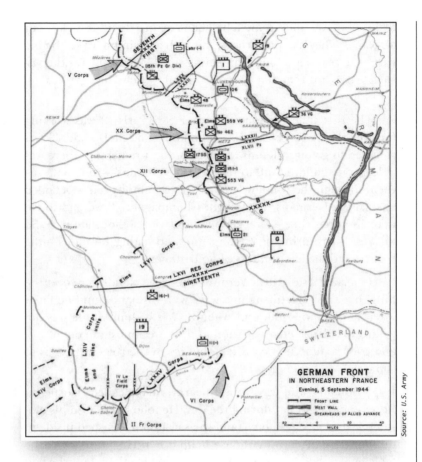

GERMAN FRONT
IN NORTHEASTERN FRANCE
Evening, 5 September 1944

Pat Patillo was his crew chief, and "Limey" was another member of the crew (he was called as such because of his affection for England, and because he'd spent so much time there). "Limey knew all the good pubs, including Dirty Dick's, and he could secure scotch for the crew when it otherwise couldn't be found," said McDonald.

The troops typically survived on K-rations and C-rations, and what McDonald calls "sawdust sausages." He would stay in the same rooms as his crew, which would have normally been frowned upon—it was considered fraternization. But in the wartime environment, certain rules were relaxed.

McDonald moved from Luxembourg to Wiesbaden, taking loads of food supplies out of Sandweiler Field in Luxembourg (now Findel Airport), where they took off downhill on the 3,400-foot strip. "As a 19-year-old, I was assigned to pick up a C-53D in Luxembourg to take to Blackpool, England, with a three-man crew. We had to take the airplane to Blackpool for its 1,000-hour inspection. And they found it had been up in a ditch, so we lost our airplane." They had done the repair with aluminum, rivets, baling wire—all manner of nonconforming stuff. McDonald was then issued a C-47 for him and his crew, and they flew "like gypsies" all over Europe.

"The first time I landed at Orly Field [Paris], I was working for the 9th Air Force Service Command," said McDonald. "I was assigned to go on to Reims to check it out. I remember there was at least one building full to the rafters with guns—you could see them through the windows—that the community had stockpiled against the Germans. We bought Champagne; all we had to eat were K-rations (like a Crackerjack box, with a chocolate bar). So we were there drinking Champagne and eating K-rations—the highest and the lowest forms of nourishment."

He related a story near Verdun, where the clouds were over the hills "like this" (gesturing in a wave with his hand), and he knew when to let down—but only when he was by himself; he was not willing to risk passengers. "Another time, we almost ran out of gas, and tried to land in a cornfield, but ice in the rows caused us to flip over."

McDonald's wife was from a nearby village called "Corne du Bois," and he met her during the war. He followed her on his motorcycle as she biked home, and she saw him but rushed inside to dinner. He went into the house behind her. His presence at the table meant that she couldn't eat, according to etiquette—she had to entertain him. After that, on her way home she would sneak through the woods to avoid him. Eventually he wore her down.

After he returned to the United States, he sent for her passage, but she couldn't get on the ship. So she went to the Pan American Airways counter at Orly in Paris, and the agent there said he was sorry, but they were booked for months. However, when she mentioned that she was going to the U.S. to be Jene's bride, it came out that the agent knew McDonald from the war, and he managed to slide her into a reserved VIP slot, for $250, on the Lockheed Constellation.

The impact from the war stayed with McDonald throughout his life. He brought home photos of the Nazi work camps that he witnessed with his own eyes, so that he could show kids at school the extent of the atrocities. So they would know and never forget.

All quotes from Jene McDonald are from the author interview.

Daffodils in Dark Days

May took up her usual station near the top of Goodwood Hill, and from its crest on the ringing June morning she could see down and across into the harbor at Portsmouth. The dogs jumped up around her and she let them go, running though the grass. The excitement shot through the air.

The rumble of engines down at the aerodrome below caught her ear first, as one Spitfire then another swung a prop then caught, sputtering to life. They assembled, ready.

Another noise came from the northeast, a steady, low grumbling at first, then with an even cadence. She turned to look over her shoulder and see the first shadowy form, the proud airplane towing its equally substantial charge. Then another. Then another. A flight of five barreled low across the downs. Each C-47 with a glider in tow. Others untethered, carrying jumpers ready for landing just a few dozen miles over the open water to the beaches of Normandy. Her heart beat hard, and she knew he was on board one of those, a paratrooper. She knew he sat huddled along the inside wall of the plane on a strap for a seat, clinging to the harness that held him and his compatriots against the bumps in the air.

The low cloud that clung to the hills to the north spread in the fresh breeze from the ocean, bringing its salt and mineral scent over the hill. The dogs played in the field laid over with tiny purple flowers in the green. Was it only a couple of months ago that he had leave and they came to this same hill to pick daffodils—resplendent, happy, yellow things in spite of the dark days. Little lights of hope in her memory. And she prayed again as each airplane and its mate strung overhead that he would make it back from that drop zone in France.

Up inside the hollow aluminum tube, like a bazooka loaded full of shot, Edward clung to the stretched canvas netting that held him fixed to his assigned spot. Seventy pounds of gear slung around him, swinging him like a pendulum each time they hit a bump in the air. Though the morning was just breaking into full light over the Channel, the heat of fear rose around him. Each one of his companions had the same mission, similar thoughts, and in a score of minutes they'd act. They'd go through that door.

He'd been up all night, but he couldn't close his eyes. He just stared ahead.

A call of alarm came from up front, even over the throbbing engines. He looked out the single window, which he could crane to see through if he twisted just right. They'd reached the coast, and fog roiled in a broth below, obscuring the target just a few hundred feet down. The sweat of constant apprehension prickled into a chill on his back. He looked to the officer two straps up, one out of the 18 men huddled in the back. The man wasn't a year his senior, and he looked solemn.

Orders were orders.

Minutes passed, and they circled once. Finally, a power reduction and Edward felt the big bird slow in the sky.

The officer signaled to the man next to the door. A turn at the upper handle, then the lower to set the two pieces free, which the infantryman secured with bungees, struggling against the airflow. The first man went out, then the next.

Edward froze in the straps. No. He thought of May. He thought of coming down on top of a glider stick. He thought of breaking his ankle. He thought of looking a German in the eye. All the things you weren't supposed to think about as you faced the door. He tried to clear his mind, but when his number came, he couldn't move.

He got a shove from the officer. Still, frozen. The man shook his head, and called to the stick next to him to go. Another shove. Still, he sat transfixed by the finality. He couldn't pull the trigger. The officer sent the men out all around him. Soon, it was the two of them, and no time left to waste. The officer drew his pistol and aimed right in his face.

"Go."

Edward blinked. The officer cocked the pistol.

He jumped out of the straps and took two big steps into the wide white world through the door.

THE D-DAY INVASION OF EUROPE MARKED a turning point in World War II, but also in the way that the C-47 was viewed by the average soldier. Jack Jackson, pilot of C-47s during this critical time, remembers that he was disappointed at first to be assigned to transport duty. "I wanted to be a fighter pilot," he said. "In a short time, though, I was delighted with the assignment, the people I flew with and served with. We flew them without any armor or armaments. It required precision flight. You had to drop troops precisely, gliders precisely. It was very demanding duty."

DATE 1944 June	AIRCRAFT MAKE	ENGINE MAKE & HORSEPOWER	FROM	TO	TYPE OR CLASS	TOTAL TIME AS CO-PILOT	TOTAL TIME SOLO-TIME-TO-DATE	SOLO FLIGHT TIME First Pilot Day	Night	Instrument	LINK	DUAL AS STUDENT Total Student	DUAL AS INSTRUCTOR Total First Pilot	REMARKS
	Make	Engine			Land	451:40	989:00	142:55	60:40			227:1	312:50	
1	C-47	R-1830-92	"P"		1		0:35	0:35					0:35	
5	C-47	"	"D" Day - France		1	1:55	5:55		4:00				2:05 / 3:55	Paratroopers
7	C-47	"			1	0:25	0:25	2						
10	C-47	"			1		2:00	2:00					2:00	
17	C-47	"			1	0:25	0:45	0:20					0:20	
24	C-47	"			3	1:50	9:45	2:35					2:35	
26	C-47	"			1	1:30	1:30							
28	C-47A	"			2	1:00	2:00	1:00					1:00	
29	C-47	"			3	1:00	2:00	1:00					1:00	
30	C-47A	"			3	1:05	2:10	1:05					1:05	
CARRY TOTALS FORWARD TO TOP OF NEXT PAGE						460:50	1010:45	5:35	145:55	60:40		227:30	325:25	PILOT'S SIGNATURE

Logbook entry of the D-Day invasion
(From the logbook of Don King, courtesy of Scott Glover)

Jackson recalled the training that allowed for the massive effort. He graduated from single-engine pilot training in April 1943. After a brief leave, he reported to Austin Bergstrom Air Force Base in Texas for his transition to the C-47, which took 30 days. "Troop Carrier Command was just getting started," Jackson said. "I was assigned to the 72nd Troop Carrier Squadron, stationed in Alliance, Nebraska, and from May to September 1943 we were training, with airborne and glider troops. We perfected the airborne drops and formation flying." Then, his unit shipped over to England, to prepare for the intense missions to come. "Through the winter of 1943 to '44, we trained—and got used to the English weather."

"Early in the morning on June 6 [1944], we took off, around 1 or 2 a.m., towing CG-4 gliders, the American gliders, to the drop zone in Normandy. The release was right at daybreak, before the beach assault. In the late afternoon, we towed British gliders, the HRSA gliders, to the landing field in Normandy—near dusk. We did one more glider run the following morning." After the initial operations, Jackson resumed supply missions, carrying everything from 5-gallon cans of gasoline, to munitions, to rations. "We were holding the front lines just as fast as they could build airstrips. Some were considered combat missions because the strips were so close to the front lines. We'd get 88mm shells at us," and sometimes took considerable enemy fire.

Jack Rickel was an infantryman brought over in late 1944 as the Allied forces fought to sustain the gains they'd made earlier that summer. "During World War II, the Fourth Infantry Division, which had been fighting since D-Day, had captured Bastogne from the Germans and were pulled back from the front lines for some deserved rest," recalled Rickel. "The Germans found out they had been replaced with new green troops from the 105th and promptly recaptured the area now known as the Battle of the Bulge.

"I was a combat infantryman replacement awaiting shipment to Europe to join the war in upstate New York, [at a location that was] then called Camp Drum. We were loaded into a British tanker, which had been converted into a troop ship for 5,000 men. It took us eight days to get to Marseille with four of the days riding out a hurricane in the mid-Atlantic. We landed at Marseille on December 23, 1944. We were given passes into the city on December 24 because they knew we were going to battle on Christmas Day.

"Early on the morning of December 25, we and all our fighting gear were loaded into 100 [C-47s]. To keep the Germans from finding out about our mini-invasion, we flew up through the Swiss Alps and then to Nancy, France. I say 'flew through the Alps' because we were at 10,000 feet and the mountains towered above us. We were seated on metal bucket seats in a row under the windows on each side of the airplane with our gear on the floor in the middle. I don't have to tell you it was *cold*.

"One by one, the [C-47s] landed at the field in Nancy; we all jumped out and ran off the runway to what little bit of shelter we could find. The field had been secured by American troops, but we were close enough to the front to hear artillery and machine-gun fire near us. We had cold K-rations for Christmas dinner. Somewhat later a convoy of trucks arrived and took us to Aachen, where we joined the Fourth Infantry Division, and within a couple of days we were engaged in retaking Bastogne, which became the Battle of the Bulge."

"I think it is doubtful that many people have seen 100 DC-3s in the air at the same time," said Rickel.

In addition to the runs that placed paratroopers and gliders at strategic locations along the front, the C-47 was also called upon to run endless supply and evacuation missions, which Jackson reported flying "on almost a daily basis." These missions formed the

Courtesy of Greg Morehead

basis for General Dwight D. Eisenhower's well-known assessment that the C-47 could be credited as one of the four tools that allowed the Allies to triumph in World War II (along with the bulldozer, the Jeep, and the "deuce and a half" truck). "Curiously enough," he said, "none of these is designed for combat."[1] The Axis forces choked on lack of logistical support, but because of the C-47's massive lifting capacity and ability to shrug off bullets and land nearly anywhere, the Allies stayed relatively well supplied. This outstanding service tipped the scales in the war, and by summer 1945, brought the fighting in Europe to a close.

As the European theater shut down, Jackson flew a C-47 along the southern route back to the United States, "across the Straits of Gibraltar and North Africa, across to Brazil and up over Puerto Rico and into Savannah, Georgia." He eventually made it back to Alliance Army Airfield, where he was to resume training in preparation for the planned invasion of Japan, in the Pacific theater of the war. "Fortunately, they dropped the bombs, and we didn't have to go." He never flew the C-47 after that.

---

1. Crusade in Europe," by Dwight D. Eisenhower
All quotes from Jack Jackson are from the author interview.
All quotes from Jack Rickel are from the author interview.

The Silent Question

re we going to make it?

It was that time in the middle, the time when the peaks stretched up sharp around them, that wore on him most during each flight. Who knew mountains could climb so high? Certainly higher than this ship, though there were few better for weight-carrying capacity and general ruggedness. He saw the pictures of the one that came back from Kunming, with the entire wingtip missing and shrapnel through the tail. Still it soldiered back to base.

But he didn't yet have a flight over that god-awful corner of creation in which he hadn't asked himself that silent question: Are we going to make it?

He'd started this tour not when he landed in Chabua but when the truck carrying him and three other freshly indoctrinated cowboys rumbled through the front gate at the base at Hondo. Texas was nowhere near the right place to train for hauling people and supplies over gross through the Himalaya— it was hot and relatively flat, and this was cold and clearly the roughest terrain on the planet. The Hump. The CBI, for "China–Burma–India." A place he vowed he'd never need talk about again as long as he lived.

Robert had picked up a C-47, with a girl named "Cookie" as nose art, earlier that day. He was now based at Myitkyina, Burma, with the 3rd Combat Cargo Group, transporting materials that had been brought to the hub within the entire theater of operations. And that ran from free China to their outposts in Burma and India, bypassing enemy territory as much as possible. But they couldn't avoid the uncharted parts of the map, where they risked their planes and cargo and lives not only against the weather and the rocks, but the unknown tribes scattered throughout the wilderness. The people that would sooner eat them than ignore them.

Dusty conditions reigned as the props constantly kicked up dirt on the airfields. Unlike back home at the base—who thought he'd ever think fondly on that base?—there was very little cement ramp area. There wasn't much civilization to speak of, in fact, except what the men brought to their brothers in the form of gallows humor and other psychological survival tactics.

His shirt and pants were the same color as the dust that covered everything else. A slight wrinkle in all because, well, where was the laundry service and an iron in the midst of the CBI theater? The silver wings with an "S" above, for "service," denoting a pilot trained on the civilian side and detailed into the Hump operations as needed. The shield with bold yet simplified stars and bars to show you were an American. A blood chit sewn into the inner lining of his jacket. Jacket the muted brown color of the camouflaged airplane in which he flew. A soldier's loose beret with a shiny dark brim.

He'd heard of fellows flying solo over the Hump and he couldn't feature it, though he knew he'd do it if he needed to. The pilot in that case sat in the right seat so as to operate all the controls; the max load was reduced to 25,000 pounds from 28,000 pounds to give better single-engine performance within the theater. He didn't want any part of that. He knew for sure that, by himself, the silent question would eat him alive.

In April 1942 the Burma Road was captured in upper Burma by the Japanese, cutting off the Allied forces from China. An aerial supply route (recommended by General Henry "Hap" Arnold) was the only logical answer. But the logistics were intense and the objective hazards to operating this supply chain were staggering.

Air Transport Command was created from the Air Ferrying Command in July 1942, with Arnold at the helm and C.R. Smith as his second in command. (Smith had been tapped to act as a general during World War II, on "loan" from his regular job leading American Airlines.) Brigadier General Earl Hoag was put in charge of the India–China Wing of the Air Transport Command, with Colonel Tom Hardin in command of Hump operations.[1]

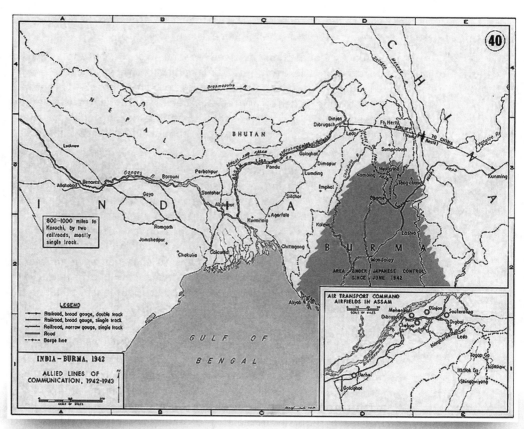

China-Burma-India
routes, 1942

Weather flying and night flying became standard operating procedure, because of the high-stakes nature of keeping China supported and ready as a base for missions against the Japanese. The result of pitting green crews against the elements with this much exposure was not hard to guess: Personnel and aircraft losses shot up. Still, under Hardin's direction, tons of material lifted over the route jumped from 4,624 in September 1943 to 23,675 in August 1944. General William Tunner replaced Hardin in September 1944, and he continued the build up: Aircraft increased from 249 airplanes to 332, with an increase in personnel from 17,032 to 22,359 by July 1945. At its height, on July 31, 1945, the India–China Wing operated 640 aircraft: 230 C-46s, 167 C-47s, 132 C-54s, 67 C-87/C-109s, 33 B-25s, 10 L-5s, and 1 B-24. The combined aircraft carried 71,042 tons of cargo over the Hump that month.

Other contributors to the efforts in this forbidding arena included the famous Chinese National Aviation Company (CNAC), the Royal Air Force, and the Royal Canadian Air Force. The CNAC had the distinction of being first to fly the Hump.

C-47 Skytrain *(Source: U.S. Air Force)*

Maj. General Claire Chennault was commander of the United States' 14th Air Force in China, and was highly respected as a pilot and leader. He was often at odds with Tunner as to which command should be the final authority in Hump operations. Yet even with this conflict, the Hump operations succeeded in their most important mission: engaging the Japanese forces in such numbers that their effectiveness and presence was curtailed elsewhere in the Pacific. American troops surely gained immensely from this situation, hastening the conclusion of the war in the Pacific.

"We flew that airlift over the highest mountains in the world," wrote Tunner in his memoir, "in good weather or bad, over large areas of territory inhabited by the enemy and by savage tribes, even head-hunters, and with a confusing variety of planes. Through this airlift, and it alone, we kept sixty-thousand American soldiers and nineteen Chinese armies sufficiently well supplied to tie down over a million and a half Japanese soldiers in China—enemy soldiers we would otherwise have had to fight in the islands of the South Pacific. All the Pacific campaigns, tough enough as they were, would have been that much more costly in American lives."[2]

Because the C-46 (Curtiss Commando) was better suited to high-altitude operations and could carry more cargo, it eventually replaced the C-47 in Hump operations. However, the C-46 suffered from maintenance and parts issues to a far greater degree than the beloved "Skytrain." The C-47s moved to their next mission—supplying British troops in India. However, the lessons learned from flying in the China–Burma–India theater would prove invaluable to other massive airlift operations, including the Berlin and Korean airlifts. The experience also solidified the importance of having a robust air transport command within the air force.

The C-47's load-carrying capability and humanitarian efforts demonstrated by Hump operations came onto center stage during the Berlin Airlift. The airlift effectively circumvented the Soviet Union's blockade of West Berlin and delivered desperately needed supplies in 1949. The Royal Air Force and United States Air Force flew more than 200,000 flights delivering more than 13,000 tons of food and fuel to civilians.[3]

The cargo-carrying ability of the C-47 combined with its range, minimal runway requirements, and toughness in the face of battle proved a powerful combination.

1. "Flying the Hump: In Original World War II Color," by Jeff Ethell and Don Downie
2. "Over The Hump," by Lt. General William H. Tunner
3. "Berlin Blockade," www.wikipedia.com, accessed on September 29, 2010

Cold Comforts

Finding a good bride was hard enough when you worked all the time, and next to impossible when that work kept you up in the woods, not seeing another human for weeks. But with the season over, and his load packed snugly on the sled, the trapper only had a couple hundred yards to get into the village to meet the airplane that would take the reindeer to market. Their antlers crossed to opposite sides of the sled to stay untangled.

Just a few miles away, the spires of evergreen loomed into the gray as the pilot steered the airplane towards the outpost's airfield, branches below like the cape sleeves of wizards. The town landing strip was cut into the timber, level and long for this place; the pilots no longer expected any more than a couple hundred feet to spare, no matter the altitude. It seems whoever was responsible for logging out the runway knew exactly when to stop to save the extra effort.

Trapping was cold, tedious work, but at least you were moving. Sitting there in the left seat, surrounded by bare metal, slicing through the air so cold it shattered, David wondered if he'd ever be warm again. It had taken them almost two hours of blowing hot kerosene air onto the big Pratts to get the oil loose enough to work its way through the engines before they could start without breaking. Kotzebue was hard on airplanes, that's for certain.

He looked on the chart, which he'd marked in red pen to call out the features he'd seen that had escaped the cartographer— who knew about oil seeps until you happened upon them? The Brooks Range was full of them. David called in range to the station manager at the outpost once he had the river leading to the airfield in sight, and John, his copilot on that flight, instinctively checked to see the cowl flaps were closed as they started the final descent. Of course they were—they hadn't been open since takeoff.

That trapper had better be ready to load when we get there. David swore he wasn't going to wait long for the old bastard—that would mean getting back to the base after dark. And the only thing colder than a winter day in Nome was a winter night there!

PIONEERING AIRLINES SUCH AS WIEN ALASKA Airlines appeared to need less infrastructure than those in the lower 48—but just because they were able to land the DC-3 on everything from gravel to glaciers, so long as the open space stretched long enough and the maintenance crew kept the airplanes in good shape. In reality, the pilots and maintenance crews needed perhaps more inner resources to brave the weather and rugged field conditions, as well as the pervasive cold that soaked the big radials and froze the hardiest of fluids in the lines if left exposed.

Doug Millard flew for Wien Alaska from 1952 to 1984, acquiring more than 5,000 hours in the DC-3. Many of Wien's aircraft were former Navy RD4s the airline had acquired from the military as they were assisting with oil exploration on the North Slope in the 1940s.

"Initially when I went on the pilots' seniority list, I was combination bush [pilot] and DC-3 copilot," said Millard. "My initial DC-3 checkout was 30 minutes familiarization in the cockpit (I had been working on them and running engines for mechanics for four years at that time) and three bounces. The next day I was a copilot on a Part 121 scheduled flight. Times do change.

"My time in the DC-3 [was] pretty routine. Oil coolers were their weak point. They would spring a leak and when the oil pressure started to drop, you would shut it down. That happened twice, as I remember. The fix was to get a long rod threaded on both ends that would reach through the cooler, cut little rubber gaskets for each end and large area washers and bolt it down to seal off the leaking core area. About the time the cooler developed its fourth leak, it was changed.

"One spring I had a charter from Nome out to Gambell on St. Lawrence Island for the Walrus festival. The plan was to take a load of Nome-ites to Gambell, drop them off, then fly to the Air Force radar site at North East Cape on the east end of the island, and

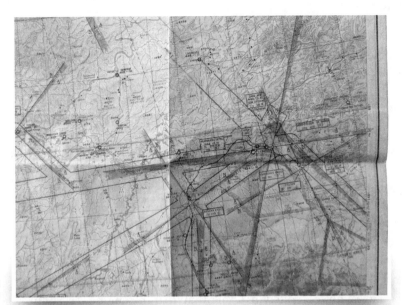

pick up a load of GIs who were waiting to attend the festival. This is the closest thing to taxi service that we have in the Alaska bush.

"When we got to Gambell and unloaded the Nome folks, I found we had a leaking oil cooler. It would have been the next day to get a mechanic from the mainland, and not wanting to disappoint the GIs at Northeast cape, not to mention the fact that there were no facilities at Gambell to house the crowd, I decided to motor over there where I knew the Air Force would have a machine shop that could thread a piece of rod and some inner tube rubber for us.

"I placed the order on the radio prior to arrival, so it didn't take long to make the repair, and the GIs were just a little late getting to the festival. Other than that, the day went off on schedule.

"Another day I was preflighting a DC-3 prior to departure from Fairbanks (I always did my own preflights whether I was flying captain or copilot), and found a leaking oil cooler. I called a mechanic to look at it and he assured me it was no problem. Two-and-a-half-hours later, we lost oil pressure and landed at Kotzebue on one engine.

"One trip from Ft. Yukon back to Fairbanks with the copilot flying, we would get one backfire from an engine each time he would make a power reduction. Other than that the engine was running like a top. On approach into Fairbanks I cautioned him not to get low and to assume we had only one engine running.

"As we taxied up toward the tower, I saw them looking at us with binoculars. I looked out at the right engine, and it was puffing out smoke every time a cylinder would fire. I pulled the mixture and we coasted in on one engine. Never did hear what the trouble was.

Millard once witnessed three men hand-prop a DC-3, as more of an experiment than out of necessity. "One man, Fritz Wien, had his left hand on the prop, his right hand was in the grasp of another man's left hand and that man's right hand was in the grasp of another man's left hand, all strung out in line. They all three gave a big tug in unison and the thing started on the first pull. The man in the cockpit has to be given a lot of credit. He had

Data plate on DC-3
in Palmer, Alaska

Wing of a DC-3 rotting in the August sun in Palmer, Alaska

given it just the right amount of prime to make it take on the first pull. Rope-starting a DC-3 [using a similar procedure as hand-propping, but with a rope in place of the human chain], while not common, was not unheard of and I had witnessed it as a kid."

Wien Alaska operated DC-3s and their variants in the state well into the 1970s, hanging onto the airplanes for roughly four decades because of their resiliency and adaptability to the remote and challenging airports scattered throughout the state. With long range and short runway capability, the only real substitutes came in the form of the Curtiss C-46 and the DC-4 Skymaster.

All quotes from Doug Millard are from the author interview.

Minks

The letter had outlined in plain-spoken type the details of her employment, as well as the first steps she would take upon arriving in New York. New York! How glamorous it all sounded. She remembered rolling over on her bed as she read the letter and laughing aloud at the precise direction, ensuring she would successfully navigate from the lodging prescribed by American to the Stewardess School at Flushing, Queens. "From the hotel take a Lexington Avenue bus south to Grand Central Station"—*Grand Central Station!*—"then the IRT subway, Flushing train (local or express) to the end of the line. Walk one-half block east on Roosevelt Avenue to the Bus Terminal Building." Then up to the third floor. Just the adventure she'd wanted!

After finishing the class, and graduating with a group of mostly swell gals—some of whom she just knew she'd keep as friends for life—she was posted to the base at New York Municipal Airport.

Her classmates always cracked that, coming from the Great Plains, there was no surprise Marge was bright and "down to earth," but she took the ribbing with a good sense of humor that she found, as she started working the line, would readily mesh with that of many cockpit crews. She had faith overall in the pilots' abilities, true, but, more importantly, she knew she could handle most anything, and those first few months on the job just grew her confidence.

Well, *most* anything.

Marge signed in for the trip that morning anticipating a regular assignment. On their way back to New York, they made a stop in Buffalo and she went into the commissary to buy a bar of chocolate that she'd been craving. Back out in the breeze, she tucked a stray hair up underneath her coffee-colored cap, and walked out across the cinders to the airplane. A dozen people came onto the Douglas and took their seats one by one. There was a little noise up front as she went to help an elderly woman in a feathered, purple hat into her seat near the bulkhead. Scratching. *That's odd.*

She was going to check on it, but felt a tap on her shoulder. The copilot, trying to get by. He smiled and she stepped into the empty row to let him pass and forgot about it. He was handsome—but not nearly the charmer that had escorted her out to dinner the last time she was in New York for the weekend. She was still mooning over *that* one. She sighed, took her place on the jumpseat, and they taxied out.

It wasn't until she was back in the galley getting out the thermoses of consommé for lunch that she recalled the noise and wondered about it. She needed to go up front in any event to get some spare silverware from the forward compartment. On her way, she noticed a worried look on the face of the woman she'd helped earlier.

"Miss, I believe there's something going on up there," the woman said, and she pointed a finger towards the front of the airplane. Guess she didn't mean the cockpit! Marge smiled, but as soon as she passed the row, she heard the scratching—and a high-pitched keening, just barely audible above the beat of the engines. She went up into the companionway and opened the door.

Immediately, the smell washed over her, knocking her back. Funky, like the dog after he rolled in a pile of manure. What on earth...?!

Marge looked into the shadowy compartment and saw the outline of several cages, and a set of dark eyes beading out at her. Immediately the metal began to rattle as the raging critters sought escape. One let out a shriek. She jumped, hoping the spindly metal frame cages would hold together.

Then she remembered. Minks. A load of the small, seemingly benign animals was on the manifest to come on board at Buffalo. But they're not supposed to be up here! And no wonder! She closed the door quickly and looked back to the first row of passengers. The woman had her nose wrinkled up, and the man next to her was staring pointedly out the window as he coughed. *Oh, dear.* Then she remembered the silverware. She opened the door again, but the cubby where she'd stashed the forks and spoons on the earlier leg was behind the cages. She tried to reach past them, but got swiped by one of the beasts. She drew her hand back, the welt raising red on her arm.

She turned and saw the woman looking at her sternly, the feather waving as she scolded Marge. "What in heaven's name do you have in that closet, Miss? It's not going to get out and eat us, is it?"

"No, ma'am. Just someone's pet." They'd just have to do without the extra silver. It wasn't a long flight to New York, anyhow. Normally. She finished the cabin service and took up her station at the front of the airplane to guard that compartment door. Every so often, when the air bumped them around, she could hear the scuttling and scratching, and it made her cringe. As long as they stayed put, she didn't want to bother the crew. But when the captain signaled for her to pass back the flight report to the passengers, he read the look on her face. "Something wrong?"

"Sir, we have minks on board." He looked puzzled. "But I think the little demons are going to stay put!" He laughed and patted her hand. "I'm sure you can handle it. But let me know if we need to dispatch any of the critters—my wife needs a new coat!" She gave him a look before relaxing into a chuckle and shaking her head.

After an eternal hour, they came into New York, touching down on Runway 1 and making the taxi over to the air terminal. Marge gave the ramp agent her best smile after coming out of the door following the last of the weary passengers, and hurried into the building. She snatched a report form from the rack and dashed off one line: "Minks should never again be brought on board an airplane." Enough said.

Margaret "Marge" Hogan Horning was a tall and slender teacher from Nebraska when she began her short career in aviation. She'd gone to Chicago to work as a secretary, and then she applied to American Airlines after seeing the newspaper advertisement for ticket agents. But a moment's mix-up led her on a different path: Instead of the hiring line for ticket agents, she wound up in the stewardess line.

She took the serendipitous turn of events in stride and, considering the prospect of flying in the DC-3s to be an adventure, eagerly entered the stewardess training class in 1944. She graduated with 41 classmates from the school in New York. In fact, New York Municipal Airport would officially become La Guardia Field during her time with the airline.

Marge was based for the most part at New York, and then for a time in Memphis, and though she was with the airline for less than five years, she had many tales to tell. For example: On a night

Stewardess school, class of 1945
(Courtesy of C.R. Smith Museum)

flight from New York to Chicago, they lost an engine early in the flight. The crew flew most of the way on one engine, making a precautionary landing in South Bend, Indiana. Imagine the explanations that she had to give to the passengers sitting on the side of the airplane with the engine feathered!

Another event: On a daytime flight from Memphis to El Paso, they ran into weather and had to put down in Salt Flats, Texas—a waypoint, but not an airport. They simply landed in the desert on a flat stretch of ground. To let the passengers off the airplane, the crew put a chair below the stairway so they could exit while waiting for a clearance into El Paso.

She entertained a number of celebrities among the passengers they carried: Dinah Shore, Gloria Swanson, Errol Flynn and "best of all," according to Marge, Donald Douglas. He gave her a memento of the DC-3: a lapel pin of the airplane, about 2½ inches in width that she wore proudly through her service for the airline.

Marge worked for American until she married; she met Hugh Horning on a flight in 1947, and they married in 1949. She accumulated more than 2,000 hours serving in the DC-3 alone, as well as on the DC-4 and DC-6. Then, according to airline policy, she had to leave employment. The no-marriage policy was not eliminated from all U.S. airlines until the early 1980s. Other requirements, such as height and weight restrictions, remain today, though for safety purposes and not for aesthetic reasons. Stewardesses on the Douglas Sleeper Transports (DSTs) had to be at least 5-feet, 5-inches tall and strong enough to leverage into place the sleeping berths that lined the cabin. The requirement to be a nurse had been dropped, as most nurses went into the military during World War II, and as the airline industry grew by leaps and bounds following the war. However, stewardesses were required to be college graduates during Marge's time at the airline.

Marge remained lifelong friends (for 60 years) with three of her roommates during her time with the airline, two in Memphis (Charlotte Hollingsworth from Flushing, and Lou Hazelton from Jamaica). They were called "The Three Hs." Marge's East Elmhurst roommate Kerry Kerrigan from Boston married an American Airlines pilot who later became chief test pilot for the company in Tulsa. The friends reunited many times over the years.

Marge Hogan Horning "flew West" on August 31, 2009, after 60 years of marriage to Hugh, and becoming mother of seven, grandmother of twelve, and great-grandmother of nine.

Adella "Dell" Follett Johnson was hired by American in 1946, a contemporary of Marge's at the airline, though the two did not know each other. Upon her hire, Dell received a letter in the mail from J.H. Baldridge, Director of Employment, outlining the initial terms:

"So that you will be thoroughly familiar with the conditions of your employment, we are briefly reviewing them for your understanding. You will be employed at a starting salary of $140 per month with further

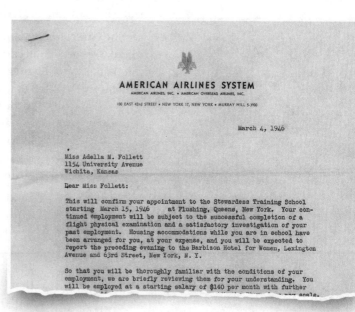

increases to $215 per month in accordance with the Stewardess pay scale. Salary checks are received on the 15th and the last day of each month and you will, therefore, be expected to have sufficient funds with you to carry you over until you receive your first paycheck. You will be expected to accept an assignment at any one of the company's base stations upon completion of your training period."

The training began with a flight physical and encompassed several weeks of familiarization with the airplanes, service equipment, and company policies. For example, stewardesses were required to fill out a report form at the end of a flight if any irregularities occurred. They served beverages and meals—but no alcohol—to the passengers. They played cards with them, and in general had a more personable experience with their passengers than we expect today.

Dell kept a detailed logbook of her flight time with American, both on the DC-3 and DC-4, as she flew routes spanning the east

Dell Follett Johnson

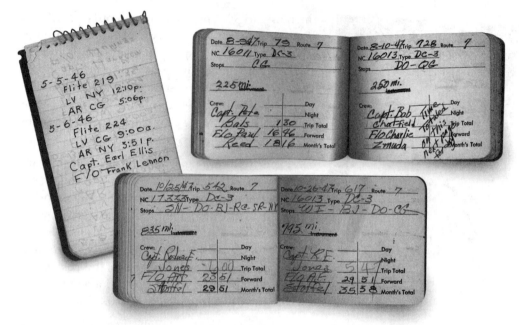

coast from New York to Chicago, and, later, from Memphis. She wrote down the names of most every captain and copilot with whom she flew, and she kept track of card scores along with these careful records. She was stewardess on the crew that opened the Springfield, Illinois, and Charleston, West Virginia, airports to commercial flights on American in 1947, and she received a letter of commendation from the company for her efforts.

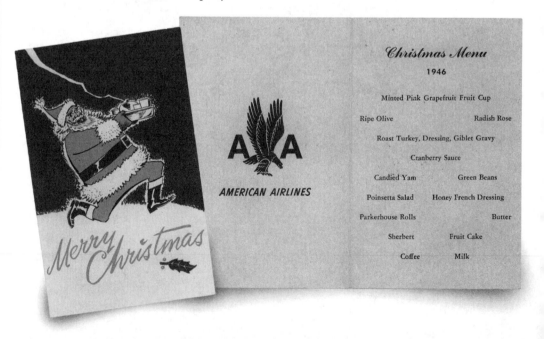

The crew had nameplates that would slide into place on the bulkhead beside the cockpit door. She kept hers, which reads "Miss A. Follett," signaling her role as the cabin crew. She also saved a single business card, a simple white card with the Flagship of the American Airlines System printed on it in blue and red. Dell resigned from the airline in 1951.

From the pages of "Service Aloft," the newsletter of the American Airlines crews, the poem "The Stewardess' Lament" satirizes the role and attitude of the stewardesses and their pilot colleagues in the sky—but there is truth in the humorous lines. These pioneering women (and men, in the case of Eastern Airlines and others who hired "stewards" as well) walked the aisle, braved a cabin that was alternately cold and hot—and always noisy—and took care of their charges with wit, grace, and a smile.

"I am the stewardess, I sit in the back
Amid pots and pans in our aerial hack;
Betimes I trip up and down the aisle,
And dutifully arrange to smile.

"Timid first-riders look trustfully at me
The blasé air travelers reach out and pat me;
A poor working girl's woes and ordeals,
Aren't in serving 21 meals.

"'Please bring me coffee' is only a ruse,
And woe to yours truly unless I vamoose;
I dispense pillows, newspapers, and such;
If the air gets too bumpy, I'll need a crutch.

"The air in the cabin's too hot or too cold,
The copilot's too young, the captain's too bold;
When I go up front to carry a tray,
Regulations provide 30 seconds to stay.

"'Tis a prudent precaution to back out and run
Before someone thinks I'm up there for fun;
And so I retreat ere scandal will brand me,
I simply must go now, 'Please sir, unhand me!'"

—Author Unknown

All quotes from Marge Hogan Horning, Hugh Horning, and Dell Johnson are from author interviews. Original source material courtesy of Hugh Horning and Dell Johnson collections.

The Last Manifest

He'd bid on the line that month knowing that they'd be among the DC-3's last in American service. As much as he wanted to move up into the new equipment, he felt a little sentimental when the sheets came out, and found his pen checking the box that would give him this last trip. The old girl might fly her last for the airline with some other captain at the controls, but not again by his hands. He was moving up to the new DC-6 for good next month. The airline had more of those sleek, four-engine planes on order, and no one could argue the -6 was faster—90 knots!—and fit his passengers' evolving expectations.

How times had changed, just in 10 years.

He'd come to the airline after the war, his hours in the C-47 serving him well for the peacetime mission. The competition for jobs was fierce, but one of his best friends in the squadron had been a chief pilot at the Memphis base for American, so he had a leg up.

The entry in the stewardess' logbook from that day: "March 4, 1948, N15579, BUF-NF-YIP-CHI; Capt. Roy Newhouse, FO John Jankowski; 3:29 total flight time."

$\sim$

As soon as the embargo on the manufacture of new aircraft for civilian use lifted in 1944, the airlines clambered to update their fleets with the newest airplanes. The DC-4 (military designation: C-54) had proven itself in the Air Transport Command, and following the war, Douglas Aircraft Company continued to build them in spite of the 500 airplanes let loose from military service, flooding the market. Airlines bought surplus C-54s to gradually replace the DC-3 on their flight lines through the close of the 1940s.

Lockheed debuted the 60-passenger *Constellation* in 1946. Douglas was at work crafting the pressurized DC-6, which would introduce an even higher level of passenger comfort than the DC-3 and DC-4 ever could. Allowing pilots to fly higher enabled them to cruise above the weather—the turbulence, wind, and, precipitation—and fly longer legs, while the passengers in the back breathed freely the pressurized cabin air, no oxygen mask required. By 1947, American had introduced the DC-6 to its fleet, and offered nonstop flights across the country. In 1948, American added the Convair 240. By the close of 1949, American's fleet consisted entirely of pressurized aircraft built after the war.

Dell's logbook showing last DC-3 entry.

The writing was on the wall for the DC-3's service for the major airlines. Eastern Airlines flew its last DC-3 in 1953; Delta Airlines' last DC-3 flight took place on October 29, 1960. Continental Airlines still operated ten DC-3s in 1960, but soon phased them out as well.

In the meantime, nonscheduled airlines began snapping up surplus C-47s and other models, converting them to passenger service, and instituting what we now think of as "coach class," the standard form of air travel for the average American today. In late 1948, the first of the scheduled airlines to promote coach fares was Capitol Airlines—quickly followed by American, and TWA. American used its DC-3s and DC-4s for this service—in the unpressurized aircraft, the lower level of service was clearly set apart from the fares traveling by day in new airplanes like the DC-6. By

1949, though, the DC-3 was phased out, and coach service between New York and Los Angeles began on the DC-6.

However, in a twist of fate, a handful of those DC-3s shaken loose by the major airlines would be picked up by wealthy and famous individuals requiring on-demand, high-end service. Yes, these second-hand silver queens would go on to carry movie stars and executives as luxury transport. Conversions were rampant following the war, with surplus C-47s going back to Douglas and other outfits for the refurbishment process.

Douglas was also (grudgingly) convinced to update the DC-3 to continue to fulfill the airlines' short-haul needs, and to this end the company produced 106 Super DC-3s. With a new wing and empennage, and more powerful Pratt & Whitney R2000 engines, the Super DC-3 had greater cargo capacity, yet it never took hold in the market like its predecessor.

Douglas Aircraft Company maintained a DC-3A as a corporate aircraft before the war, N30000, a Douglas Executive model. That registration number was later used on a Super DC-3.

Stewardess' logbook entry from Dell Johnson collection.

The Frontiers

She hoped as she looked through the flakes into the snow-darkened sky that she would soon hear the engines that signaled to her that her girl might have a chance. The husky had come out of nowhere—you never could fully trust the ones that still had a streak of wolf in them. Left Missy in such a state, not just with angry claw marks covering her chest and legs, but her arm twisted back into a crook. What scared her most was the contusion on her forehead, and the blood that wouldn't stop streaming down Missy's six-year-old face. They'd quickly bandaged her as best they could and cradled her in the front cab of the old orange Ford for the short drive to the airport.

She recalled the summer with its long days, and the giant squash that grew in her yard, soaking up the sun. Outsized, making up for lost time, for the sparse collection of its neighbors. She had to can it quickly, to save the summer for the winter. But now, she'd trade every jar of it stacked in the cellar for a clear sky this afternoon.

A couple miles west of town, the scrub opened up to reveal a broad runway. They pulled up to the airport office to find the station manager coming out the door to meet them.

"How's our little one?" he asked. "I just called in and got an FAA airplane that had been over to King Salmon...they're going to stop here on their way back to base."

As he said it, she could hear the engines in the distance, with no wind to drown out the sound. The airplane flew over the field, and then came in to a soft landing on the runway, then stopped, turned, and looked like it was taxiing back to get to the ramp. All of a sudden, the airplane stopped again, and the cargo door opened.

"Get back in the car, let's drive out there," the manager said, now figuring the airplane wouldn't take the time to taxi in. She got back in the truck and scooted over to let him start the engine. As they sped out to the runway, she thought she saw through the snow several large shapes being pushed out of the door of the airplane into the soft shoulder of the runway. "What are they doing?"

The station manager slowed as he approached the airplane. "I reckon they're making room for you." He put the truck into park and got out to talk with the man silhouetted in the cargo door.

She got out, cradling the girl in her arms, and she walked as quickly and gently as she could to the gaping door. "Careful!!" she cried, as she lifted Missy into waiting arms. She lifted herself up the steps next, tears coming down with relief. She might make it. That little girl just might make it now.

ELVIN JACKSON SPENT AN IMPORTANT PORTION of his career flying for the FAA in Alaska. He spoke reverently of Jack Jefford, who led the efforts of the Civil Aviation Authority (and after 1958, when the CAA became the Federal Aviation Administration, the FAA) in Alaska. Jefford was perhaps the first to really see the big picture—that the state would gain exponentially from the development of a proper infrastructure suited to its needs—which diverged significantly in some areas from those of civil aviation in the coterminous United States. The agency operated a series of DC-3s in its mission of developing airfields and radio navigation, including the first one, known as "King Chris," registered as NC-14 (c/n 4080), a DC-3A-348 purchased new by the CAA for $119,000. The airplane was the first of several DC-3s and other larger aircraft that would take the place of the short-range planes and allow the agency to serve the Aleutian Islands during World War II.[1]

Jackson had been up north for most of his life, and he flew several aircraft over the course of his career with the CAA/FAA in Alaska, as the agency continued to open up instrument flying in the frontier through the 1960s. While DC-3s were used as flight check aircraft all over the United States, their role persisted in Alaska because of the environment's unique demands. The CAA had begun operating the DC-3 in 1941, but began flight inspection with the airplane at some point following the war, around 1950.[2]

Elvin Jackson

A large percentage of Jackson's flying was routine, from an operational perspective. He related just a few events that stood out from his time with the DC-3. "I never had to feather an engine in flight other than on training and proficiency flights which will attest to the reliability of those PW 1830–94 engines. Also during that time, other than one fatal crash in one of our Flight Inspection DC-3 aircraft that killed two of our pilots, the Anchorage FIDO, Flight Inspection District Office, did not have any accidents.

"Sure, there were a number of times when I was called upon to deviate from the work being accomplished to respond to an emergency.

"We made a DC-3 logistic flight into the FAA station at King Salmon, Alaska. For the return flight, the station had a load of appliances for redistribution. After takeoff, we received a call from the Iliamna FAA station requesting that we deviate over to that station and pick up a little three-year-old girl (who had gotten too close to a tied-up husky dog and was badly mauled) along with her mother and take them into Anchorage.

"As the plane was so loaded, we couldn't get one of the seats down so just taxied over to one side of the runway, opened the cargo doors and literally kicked out enough of those old appliances to get a seat down, took them aboard and headed for Anchorage with a call to have an ambulance waiting. We kept a little more than cruise power on the engines all the way back to Anchorage and, I think, [set] a record from Iliamna to Anchorage in a DC-3." The little girl survived because of their efforts.

"There was the time when we made an R-O-N [overnight] in Fairbanks when it was forty below [zero], and the next morning it was fifty-two below. It took several hours with Herman Nelson heaters to get the engines warm enough to turn a prop [for] when we got ready to depart on our flight inspection mission.

Former CAA DC-3 at Palmer, Alaska

"I ran up the engines in place and everything checked out, but after taxiing down to the end of the runway, I made another run up, and this time when the feather button was punched in, nothing happened on either engine. It was either go back and put the heat on again, but then the same thing would probably happen, or take off and pray that we didn't have an engine failure, in which case we'd—no doubt—buy the farm. I looked over at my copilot and said, 'Ken, what do you think?' His reply: 'I'm with you,' so we took off, got the work done, and headed home to Anchorage."

Chart of Alaska from 1950s showing portion of Fairbanks to Nome route

Other interesting stories centered around the airplane's utility in extreme conditions, and the FAA's operations in remote areas. "Once while doing some flight check work on St. Lawrence Island [in the Bering Sea], we received a call from the Nome FAA flight service station requesting that I contact the Eskimo village at Savoonga [on St. Lawrence Island], and he gave me a frequency.

"After making contact with the village, I was told that they had an Eskimo man who had been delirious and out of his head for three days. They wanted to know if we could land and take this man into Nome to the hospital. At that time it was snowing quite heavily, so I made a low pass over the runway to check the conditions of it. We didn't like what we saw, as the wind was blowing snow across the runway, and it had some pretty good snow drifts along the length of it, not having been plowed.

"I pulled up, looked over at my copilot, and said, 'Well, Bill, what do you think?' His reply: 'You're the PIC, pilot-in-command.' I sure hated not landing and taking this poor fellow to Nome, so my reply was, 'Let's do it.' We made the approach, set it down on the end of the strip and, fortunately, those drifts were fairly soft and the wheels just plowed through them.

"The natives brought the fellow down on a blanket with six [of them] holding on to it. We always carried a stretcher in the plane, so we laid the fellow on it, put several straps across him plus strapped the stretcher down, and took him into Nome, where they had an ambulance waiting."

Tom Gribble also flew the DC-3 while working in Alaska for the FAA. He recalled, "When parked overnight in Southeastern Alaska (Ketchikan comes easily to mind), wind-driven rain would get in the "P" leads or ignition harness. They sometimes had to be blown out before starting. For some reason, there was never a problem in flight. And, yes, we did get wet in the cockpit while flying in rain.

"When the FAA had a large fleet of Dougs—55 flight check aircraft (plus another six as administrative or logistic aircraft) in 1961—the agency had its own overhaul shop in Oklahoma City. Those folks, I'm told, did outstanding work and the engines were very reliable.

"With only 1,056 hours in the DC-3, I've had three engine failures. Of course, all three aircraft had been flown thousands of hours without a failure; I just happened to be on the spot when the isolated events occurred. Only one would be considered a catastrophic failure. I was a very low-time copilot for an oil company flying one of only three (at the time) civilian Super DC-3s, same as the Navy's R4D-8. The DC-3S is powered by 1475-horsepower, nine-cylinder Wright R-1820-82 Cyclone engines. One dark midnight we blew a large hole in the head of one cylinder on the right side and pumped all the oil out before we got it feathered. The engine seized."

The airplane was also used in developmental work in remote locations for the FAA elsewhere in the world. Cal Franklin flew for the FAA in the Middle East and Africa in the DC-3, mostly checking navaids. His basic training in the -3 was with the FAA, who sent down a check pilot to both give him the type rating and check airman status. Cal was then in the Middle East and North Africa for 2½ years. Once in Africa, he was promoted to chief pilot and served in that role for 18 to 20 months.

One "moment of terror" that was "self-inflicted" happened during this time period. He was with three pilots, flying out of Addis Ababa, Ethiopia, which is surrounded by 8,500-foot terrain, in a C-47, which has a roughly 6,000-foot single-engine service ceiling (manuals say 12,500 is absolute single-engine service ceiling, with 200 FPM observed at 6,300 feet). They were flying at 12,500 feet MSL when a hydraulic line broke in the "Christmas tree."

To back up a step, this C-47 had been an Allegheny Airlines airplane that was delivered to Addis with maintenance technicians. Franklin took it for the acceptance flight, and this was the result. They landed back at Addis with hydraulic fluid still pumping out—at the old airport (the new one was built for the jets), from which they still operated DC-3s locally.

Then on the second flight, another hydraulic line broke. Ethiopian Airlines made him three flex lines to put within the aluminum casings. One of those had broken, and it had pumped out five gallons. He and the other three pilots on board decided to shut down the engine on that side and feather the prop to take pressure off the line. After shutting it down, Franklin went to work on disassembling and reattaching the line.

After a bit, the guy flying said, "Cal, you'd better hurry," because they were drifting down, and the surrounding terrain loomed all around. The airplane got as low as about 600 feet AGL before they got the engine back up and running. So that one was self-inflicted, because they didn't have to shut down and feather a perfectly good engine.

Another incident that happened while he was in Addis: He was hit in the back of the head with a hailstone—as it turns out, the window slides, and on the back side there's felt packing around the window glass, and the felt had just about worn through, so the window had a gap big enough to let a pea-sized hailstone through.

Once he returned to the U.S., Franklin worked as a charter and contract pilot on the DC-3, Convair 240, 340, and 440, and the Jet Commander 21, 22, 23, 24. He flew the Atlanta Hawks when the team came to Atlanta in the early 1980s.

Franklin recalled another DC-3 episode: He was flying from North Carolina to Atlanta, and he was on final for Runway 33 at Atlanta Hartsfield airport in the midst of a thunderstorm. He had lowered the left seat so that he wouldn't be blinded by the flashes of lightning while flying the ILS. The copilot in his nervousness had lowered the spades first on the gear, hanging up the works. So Franklin had to go in there, while on final (because they were not going to go around) and re-sequence the gear, all the while flying the glideslope/localizer needles. He later found out the flight attendant had come in during that time to see how close they were to landing, and "saw the Chinese fire drill going on" and left the cockpit quickly. Once the pressure came to 1,000 psi and he neutralized the handle, he came to minimums (altitude and visibility) and saw the runway lights.

He flew the "Hyper 3"—same as a Super 3, with the "big engines, and extended rudder," used in cargo operations. It was later sold to Helmut Weiner, and he took it out to Hayward. He says that the Hyper 3 "saved my life—or a big embarrassment."

He flew the airplane out to Hayward, as the chief pilot, and had to fly it with an FAA representative who wanted to see him calculate a drift-down plan (using single-engine performance figures). He was flying copies of the *Wall Street Journal* from Hayward and Redwood to Reno, and all the routes were above the single-engine service ceiling, hence the call for the drift-down plan. He didn't have one—he had never really done that. But in the Hyper 3, the single-engine service ceiling was higher than that of the standard DC-3, so it was in the ops manual, and he figured it out and told the FAA guy that the drift-down plan wasn't required.

Franklin also described the "rudder lock" feature on the DC-3: "You can slow the aircraft almost to V_{MC} (about 86 to 87 knots) and push in the rudder all the way slowly, and when at full deflection, you can feel it go over "a little clunk" and you can take your feet off. You just push in on the other rudder pedal to unlock it." More unique features on a unique airplane.

1. "Winging It!" by Jack Jefford
2. "Flight Check!: The Story of FAA Flight Inspection," by Scott A. Thompson
All quotes from Elvin Jackson, Tom Gribble, and Cal Franklin are from author interviews.

Captured

Emily turned the ticket envelope over in her hands, which was bright green with a DC-3 flying high over a cowboy on the front. Sure, she was looking forward to the weekend—but she really looked forward to the flight, her very first.

The winter morning was clear and beautiful, with snow sprinkling the foothills west of Denver. Arriving at Stapleton Airfield, she pulled her wool coat around herself more closely as she walked below the words proclaiming "Denver Air Terminal," after her father and brother brought her there. Emily rose an eyebrow when her father bought life insurance on her for the trip from a machine in the terminal, but it didn't deter her from wanting to go.

She was directed out to the airplane with the grand, forest green logo for Frontier Airlines on the tail and nose, stylized to look like an "F" in reverse, or a feather atop the arrow. A stewardess greeted her at the door and she made her way to her seat inside. She'd seen them come by the cosmetics counter at the May Company where she worked in downtown Denver, all kitted out in uniform, and their adventurous lives intrigued her. She wondered for a moment how she would do as a stewardess herself...it had sounded so much more interesting than nursing! That's what her twin sister, Eileen, hoped to do—but she had cautioned her that she couldn't see Emily as a nurse. Eileen was right about that.

Within a few minutes, the whole airplane shook as one engine came to life. She could see the blades blur into a streak from her seat, and she could feel every crack in the pavement as they taxied out to the north/south runway. The takeoff from Denver took them to the north, and her heart leaped at the captain's first bank to point them southward towards Pueblo.

At that stop, Emily got out of the airplane and walked around a bit on the ramp. She snapped a picture of the DC-3 in which she'd just flown. Soon, they were back inside, and climbing hard to make it across the Continental Divide, over Monarch Pass, into Gunnison. She looked out at the peaks she knew climbed to more than 14,000 feet—there was Blanca, perhaps, standing out at the end of the Sangre de Cristos? It slid past her window. How would you know how high you were without those mountains to guide you?

A sharp touchdown at Gunnison's airport, and the airplane pitched back as they rolled to a stop on the runway. With a fire of the engines that thrilled her again, they turned around and taxied in. Well, most girls would suffer many things for a getaway weekend with friends far from home, but she was a little sad to have the flight itself end.

She knew she had the return trip, though, on Monday, and she woke early to meet the airplane that would take her home. No other takers on this flight, though; she was the sole passenger boarding the little stairs into the cabin. The long takeoff roll opened her eyes a bit, as she watched the hills of the Gunnison Valley slide right underneath them, but then she recognized the college as they banked over town to climb up high enough to make it over the pass.

The airplane leveled off, and she felt the timbre of the engines and props descend in pitch. They must not need as much power to stay aloft as they do to climb. Emily gazed out the window, thinking, when the stewardess came by to see if she wanted anything.

"Gee, do you think I could see the cockpit?" The stewardess went to check, and then came back with a "yes."

Emily unbuckled her lap belt and followed the young woman up front. With a gesture, she invited her to enter the narrow space that led to the front-row seats. The two men up front sat relaxed, comfortable, enjoying the fine day, and greeted her, showing her how the jumpseat lifted up into place. She sat there, transfixed, for the ride back to Denver, watching as the pair managed the engines with three sets of levers in the center console, and updated their course on the navigation radios. One of the pilots explained the airspeed indicator, altimeter, and vertical speed indicator on the panel, showing their climb and descent. The copilot called into Denver when they were still many miles away—when she could just barely see the city's outline on the horizon.

Later, she thought of a hundred questions she forgot to ask, but she knew she'd peppered the pilots then with as many as came to mind. Flying was this amazing thing she had never dreamed of, yet it felt so instantly real to her. She had to be a part of it. She had to sit up front.

THOUGH HELEN RICHEY WAS OFFICIALLY THE first woman to fly for a commercial airline, her experience in 1934 was short-lived, and she was never allowed to truly join the ranks of her fellow pilots. Emily Howell Warner was the first woman to truly "fly the line," joining Frontier Airlines as a pilot (already having amassed more than 7,000 hours) in January 1973. The spark that drove Warner to persist in her pursuit of this dream started with a DC-3—a Frontier DC-3.

"I have a twin sister, she wanted to be a nurse, and when I was out of high school I was going to go with her," said Warner. "She said, 'Emily, being a nurse is not for you.' I was working at the old May Company [department store] in Denver, and the flight attendants used to come through and buy stuff, and they came through in uniform. They looked so glamorous and they got to travel. You had to be 20-and-a-half in order to apply—I figured because they served liquor on the airplane, so I had some time to wait. I was 18 or 19 at the time. One of the girls had a daughter going to Western State College in Gunnison and she asked me, 'Have you ever flown before?' I said I think I would [like it].

"I bought a ticket on Frontier; they had DC-3s then. It was January 1959 and I still have the original ticket. The flight went

The Frontier Airlines DC-3 in which Emily Howell Warner took her first flight. *(Courtesy of Emily Howell Warner)*

through Pueblo to Gunnison, and I didn't get airsick, that was a good step. I was looking forward to the weekend [visit to Gunnison] because there was a dance. I had a great weekend! I came back in the early morning. I got on board, and I was the only one on the airplane on the way back to Denver. I was talking to the stewardess and said I'd like to see the cockpit. Back then, security was not an issue.

"I went forward into the cockpit, and I was just floored at what I saw. It just grabbed me; we were just coming over the mountains. It looked so different from the front. I sat in the jumpseat, and rode on the jumpseat all the way back to Denver. I was just awed by the whole thing. I didn't have a driver's license yet, and there was no one there to pick me up when I got home, so I had to take the bus home, and I went to the bus stop to wait. Ironically, the copilot saw me standing there, and gave me a ride over to Colfax [Avenue], and I was just jabbering about flying. He said, 'Gee, if you want to fly, why don't you take flying lessons?'"

"Can a girl take lessons?" she asked. When she heard in the affirmative, she made her way to Clinton Aviation, on the field at Stapleton Airport, and began flying in a Cessna 140. It would take her another 15 years before Frontier would hire her as a pilot. But that first flight in a DC-3 cemented the path that would take her there.

Frontier ticket jacket for Warner's first flight.
(Courtesy of Emily Howell Warner)

Frontier Airlines expanded throughout the 1960s, and the DC-3 was an important factor in the airline's early growth, followed by the Convair 580, introduced in June 1964. By 1968, Frontier had retired all of its DC-3s. It was while flying for Frontier that the airplane once again proved its ability to withstand severe pain and soldier on: During a flight from Prescott to Phoenix, across the New River Mountains in Arizona, a Frontier DC-3 hit terrain while recovering from a severe downdraft in deteriorating weather conditions. The impact sheared off roughly nine feet of the left wing—but the pilot maintained control of the airplane and it limped the 37 remaining miles into Phoenix safely.

Julie Clark has fond memories of Southwest Airways, and first flights that also set the stage for her future career as a pilot: Her father, Ernie Clark, was one of the founders of the California airline, one of the original 30 pilots (all captains)—the "Dirty 30" who got the airline off the ground.

Southwest Airways was founded in late 1946 at Long Beach (LGB) airport, and in 1958 moved to San Francisco International Airport (SFO), and became Pacific Air Lines. In 1968, it merged with West Coast and Bonanza to become Air West. Howard Hughes bought the airline in 1970 and it became Hughes Air West. Julie was hired by Hughes Air West as her first airline job. It merged into Republic Airlines in 1980, and then Republic was absorbed by Northwest, which Julie retired from in 2003, flying the Airbus. She had flown the DC-9 as well during her time at Northwest.

Julie, also an accomplished airshow pilot, took her very first flight in the DC-3 as a 3-month-old toddler, along with her mother, twin sister, and older sister, in 1948. Her dad was flying; they had to shut one engine down, though she does not recall that flight. She first flew with her father (that she can recall) in the mid-1950s in a DC-3, and she just adored him and wanted to be there.

Ernie was one of the Southwest Airways pilots to conduct experimental flights into Eureka–Arcata airport in Northern California on the coast, where fog was so pervasive it was the norm rather than the exception. The company experimented with smudge pots to break up the fog and allow for landings during the worst times. With its slow approach speed and flexibility, the DC-3 was a great platform for these tests.

DC-3 into Eureka, with smudge pots.
(Courtesy of Julie Clark)

Weather Bound

The curtain of gray came down to the horizon, leaving just a few miles' visibility under the cloud layer. Rows of low clouds like dollops of whipped cream marched below, maybe 300 or 400 feet above the fields just starting to green. They were level at 3,500 feet, eastbound, having departed Des Moines in visual conditions. He could see the track over the ground trail under the nose, which was cocked almost 30 degrees into the north wind. The pair started the day yesterday in St. Louis, with other stops at Quincy, Burlington, and Ottumwa, and with a layover in Des Moines.

Summer would still take a couple of months to get here, that's for sure, he thought. Winter always has one more cold shot to give you. "We'd better give them a call," he said to Bob, in the right seat.

Bob keyed the mike to pick up the clearance that he knew now would be necessary. "Chicago Center, Ozark four-six-oh, would like to pick up an IFR clearance from you."

"Ozark four-six-oh, say position." It sounded like the center controller had to put down his coffee. Things might start to get busy if a bunch of guys needed pick-ups.

"Ozark four-six-oh is 20 east of the Des Moines VOR, level 3,500."

"Okay, Ozark four-six-oh, maintain VFR and standby." Glen looked out ahead and could make out less and less of the ground in front of the airplane. This was going to be a challenge. He took a ten-degree heading change without thinking about it to aim for light sky. Okay, when's this guy getting back to us?

The visibility suddenly dropped to nothing, and the gray enveloped them for just a few seconds. He brought the nose down a bit to stay visual under the layer, which was clearly descending now. The minutes stretched. He had a little altitude to work with here, to stay above the minimums for the quadrant, but not a whole lot. A little rain spattered the windshield, and he reached up to twist the knob to clear it once with the wipers.

"Ozark four-six-oh, ready to copy?"

"Affirmative, four-six-oh."

"Ozark four-six-oh is cleared to the Iowa City airport via Victor Six, direct NASAL intersection, Victor Six direct to the Iowa City VOR, maintain 5,000. Report NASAL." Bob had already tuned in the Cedar Rapids VOR so they could ID the intersection, and he read back the clearance to the controller.

"Readback correct. And what's your fuel on board?"

"We have three hours, Ozark four-six-oh." Glen eased back on the yoke and sighed as they immediately entered the cloud deck. More rain on the windshield. With the short flight to Iowa City he wasn't too concerned, but sometimes after a spell this particular airframe seemed to leak just enough rainwater into the avionics bay in the nose to flicker the lights on the panel.

Bob tuned in 116.2 to raise the Iowa City VOR, for the approach to Runway 35, and turned up the volume in the headset to hear the "dot-dot-dot; dash-dash-dash; dot-dash-dash" of the Morse code identifier for the station. It came through clear; they were less than 40 miles out.

No need to descend much prior to the fix; one letdown to 2,600 feet msl, and they were soon making the procedure turn and lining up northbound. Glen knew the course was offset about 10 degrees from the runway, the shortest at the airport but still long enough for them. With any luck we'll break out with enough room to circle to 30, he thought.

Sure enough, as they put down the gear at the VOR, and started in the 6 miles to the airport, Bob had no sooner marked the time on the clock than the layers of scud began presenting themselves again. Two miles out, Bob called the field in sight, and Glen made a right turn to line up for Runway 30. The wet pavement rewarded good technique with an extra-smooth touchdown, and within a minute or two they taxied up in front of the terminal, with the old United "drive-thru" hangar in the background.

The passengers came out of the door on the right side of the fuselage after the blades on that side stopped turning, and Glen had a few moments to ponder the old hangar. Back in the 1920s, United had taxied its airplanes right into the open bay, allowing its passengers to deplane out of the weather. Funny how they weren't serving folks better in that regard today, but the DC-3 was just too tall to taxi in, he thought. Maybe.

The station manager tucked a new bag of mail into the rear cargo bin, and handed the manifest to the stewardess after the three new passengers got on board. The manager tucked a 3 x 5 card in his vest and hollered up towards the cockpit, "All ready, folks!"

Glen fired up the left engine again, and, with the stewardess giving the cabin briefing as they taxied out, they were off to Moline.

BEFORE THE OZARK AIRLINES FAMILIAR TO most began service, two other operations had carried the name, one in the early 1930s, and the second during World War II. On September 26, 1950, using a DC-3 acquired from Parks Airlines, the penultimate Ozark Airlines marked its first flight, from St. Louis to Chicago, with a stop in Decatur, Illinois, carrying one passenger. Serving up to 52 cities in ten states, Ozark covered the central United States using the DC-3 as the mainstay of its fleet through the 1950s and 1960s.[1]

DC-3 in front of the Iowa City terminal
(Courtesy of Jay Honeck)

Former Ozark pilot Ed Leek recalled how the airplane served the region: "Ozark Airlines (home office and base in St. Louis) owned [several DC-3s] from the mid to late 1950s until it was traded as part of a deal for a new fleet of FH–227B and DC-9 aircraft in late 1968.

"Ozark owned a fleet of 31 DC-3s numbered from N128D through N151D. (They also had N9124R, N9184, N163J through N166J, plus N52V.) N52V was a military C-47 purchased in freighter configuration and used as that only. N163J was also later converted from a passenger DC-3 to freighter configuration, as it was a very successful endeavor. Our motto was 'Go Getters go Ozark,' and we named the freighters 'Cargo Getters.'

N143D (c/n 2054, re-registered in the U.S.) in Ozark livery. *(Courtesy of Dan Gryder)*

"I began my airline career with Ozark in St. Louis on April 4, 1960. I first flew N143D on May 15, 1960, and last flew it, according to my logbooks, on May 2, 1966. I purposely commuted to fly the final runs Ozark used the DC-3 on, and my last DC-3 flight was on September 2, 1968 (on N133D). I amassed about 6,000 hours in them and was originally checked out as a captain in one of them (N131D) on February 22, 1966.

"All of the 'D' series aircraft (N128D through N151D) had the speed upgrade using [the following]: wheel clamshell doors, aileron gap filler strips, reduced size wing fillets, second auxiliary fuel tank removed, and identical standardized panels, among other items. We flight planned them at 148 knots, and they had no problem in achieving that cruise speed. We figured for flight planning a fuel burn of 100 gph, but in reality it was closer to 90 gph, which made it possible to have a little extra range if needed due to weather (which in Iowa, Missouri, and Illinois there was plenty all year round).

"The DC-3 was, and is still, one of my favorite aircraft. If fuel were not so costly, I would own one now that I am retired."

The DC-3 spurred growth for many domestic airlines during the 1950s and 1960s, as the major airlines shed their fleets. North Central Airlines evolved out of Wisconsin Central Airlines, which had launched in May 1944 and started intrastate service in 1946 with two Cessna Bobcats. The airline acquired its first six DC-3s from TWA in early 1951. It operated 32 DC-3s by 1958, connecting cities across the upper midwest, stretching from Chicago's Midway to Fargo, North Dakota. The final flight of the DC-3 in North Central service was on February 7, 1969, from Mankato to Minneapolis, Minnesota. However, the company kept one DC-3, N21728, to use for executive transport. It was retired with

Ozark DC-3 checklist

more than 85,000 hours, to the Henry Ford Museum in Detroit, Michigan.[2]

Paul Weill worked in line maintenance for North Central Airlines starting in January 1958, and continued with the airline through several mergers, ending his career there after 36 years. Weill recalled why the airline chose to keep to the Wright 1820s. "When Wisconsin Central [predecessor to North Central Airlines] needed a larger aircraft than the Lockheed 10A, they went shopping for DC-3s. TWA had some available, so they were purchased. These were equipped with the Wright 1820s. The next batch were from Eastern, also with 1820s. To keep the fleet uniform, all others [they] bought had the Wrights.

"The 1820 is a snappier engine than the 1830. The 1830 is a much smoother-running engine. With more vibration created by the 1820s, the wing-to-fuselage attach angles were more vulnerable to cracking. These were carefully inspected each maintenance check. I believe an AD [airworthiness directive] note was issued after a [significant] crash. To replace an attach angle was major, [and] down time was quite long, better than a week. The overhaul time for the 1820 was [set at] 1,200 hours.

"The 3's maintenance was basically [a succession of] A, B, and C checks; these were accomplished at various time periods. The airframe would go through an overhaul at 12,500 hours. An aircraft would arrive at the maintenance dock, [and] would be inspected, worked on, and generally out the door in one to two days." With such tight turnaround times, the technicians had to be expert at the airplane—and be able to readily fix any problem. The building blocks of the DC-3's construction allowed for this: There were few truly expensive or specialized parts, and mechanics could re-create much of the aluminum work if required.

Even the big radial engines were built to withstand multiple overhauls over a long lifetime. "During World War II, the Studebaker car manufacturer produced a lot of these engines," said Weill. "They were used on the B-17 and other aircraft. We at

Ozark DC-3 (N143D) with North Central Convair at Midway airport in Chicago.
(Courtesy of American Aviation Historical Society)

North Central did not overhaul the engines in house, but [they] were sent to Gopher Aviation in Rochester, Minnesota. The bare engine with the mags was overhauled and returned, then the engine shop would build them up." North Central used the Wright 1820s on its DC-3s for another good reason: The 1830s had a two-stage blower for high-altitude operations—an additional maintenance item that was unnecessary, given the low-altitude route structure North Central maintained.

The standard North Central DC-3 was configured with 26 seats (a handful of ex-Navy aircraft in the fleet had 28 seats); boots on wings and horizontal stabilizer; and alcohol-deiced props, carburetor and windshield. The airline used three tanks of 200 gallons apiece, with only a main tank on the right side.

Flights operated under visual flight rules, staying in the clear unless instrument conditions prevailed. Pilots made position reports through their own dispatch via high-frequency (HF) radio or the nearest North Central ground station when flying visually. Pilots flew at altitudes from 3,500 to 5,500 feet for most flights. North Central operated a series of ADF stations that the airline was authorized to use for instrument approaches in areas not yet served by VOR or federal ADF stations. These ADF stations also formed "NCA routes" indicated by light brown lines on the Jepp charts used by pilots. The airplane has witnessed this transition through several generations of navigation aids—the radio range, ADF, VOR, ILS, and now GPS—and taken each innovation in stride. Swap out the avionics in the instrument panel, install the right antenna, and the next greatest technology is ready for the DC-3.

1. www.ozarkairlines.com (Ozark Airlines history website, accessed September 20, 2010)
2. www.hermantheduck.org (North Central Airlines history website, accessed September 20, 2010)
All quotes from Ed Leek and Paul Weill are from author interviews.

Puff

After more than four hours in the air, the night had settled around them like a cloak. But Airman First Class Levitow knew the line of fire in the sky that the tracers drew as they made each circuit. Another guy in the unit had taken a time-lapse picture of one of the C–47s as it circled not far from the base. A mesmerizing sight, if the reality of their mission wasn't so horrifying.

Major Carpenter, commanding the AC–47, saw the muzzle flashes first out of the cockpit's side window over to the south and east as they circled the base. Clearly it was hot enough to go in, so he took up an attack position, circling the area of activity. His finger on the trigger, he signaled to the men in back that he would begin fire momentarily, so that they would be ready to reload.

A thousand rounds...two thousand rounds...they laid it on those devils below pretty thick. After a second pass over the target, he got the word to set up for flares, in order to give the ground troops coming in more light from the sky.

With a new command from Carpenter, Levitow started into setting the ignition and ejection controls on the flares. He handed one to Sergeant Owen, who took the flare from him like a newborn baby and hooked it onto the lanyard. Though the Pratts rumbled ahead, he could hear the roar of the mortar fire steadily increase even above the general din of the gun-ship. This was not good.

He leaned into the turn without thinking as Carpenter swung around to face a new target. Suddenly, the percussion of a direct hit rocked the cabin and sent him across the floor, and the airplane sunk as though it was falling off a cliff. Metal flew all around. When the shrapnel hit his back, it knocked him like a two-by-four. After shaking off the initial impact, he saw Owen sliding dangerously close to the open cargo door. He crawled over to pull his buddy to relative safety.

Up front, the crew wondered for a moment where they'd been hit, but the immediate task was keeping the airplane upright. So heavy on the right wing. Carpenter felt it as he racked the yoke over to the left to countermand the upset.

The hits to his body notwithstanding, Levitow saw the flare they'd been prepping roll off to the side of the cabin. He had 20 seconds between arming it and when the sucker would ignite. He knew it would burn at 4,000 degrees and fill the cabin with toxic smoke. He didn't think about what he had to do—he just did it.

With sheer will to overcome extreme pain, he dragged himself toward the flare and grabbed it as it rolled on the floor. Using his damaged body as best he could, smearing blood like the path of a snail, he made it to the open door where he could push the flare through the opening.

The flare fell away into the dark, igniting white like a flashbulb as it exploded.

The DC-3's military versions took on many forms, and not all of them in the cargo ("C") or troop carrier ("TC") role. The airplane also mastered an "AC" or attack role as the AC-47. First introduced in 1965, all AC-47s were conversions to the model from C-47s. The AC-47 was the United States Air Force's first operational gunship. During the Vietnam War, the AC-47 flew several hundred missions over Southeast Asia, in reconnaissance and attack, and as aerial support to ground troops and truck convoys.

The AC-47 was also used in psychological warfare ("psy ops") during the conflict, spreading leaflets and voice messages throughout the region. Anthony Sharp recalled dropping leaflets in Southeast Asia from an AC-47 during 1967 and 1968. The "Spooky" gunship missions lasted through 1969. Crew affectionately referred to the airplane as "Puff the Magic Dragon," based on its propensity to surround itself with the smoke of gunfire.

One of the last missions took the callsign Spooky 71. The mission began in early evening and ended around midnight on February 24, 1969. The airplane was an AC-47D detailed to the 3rd Special Operations Squadron, 14th Special Operations Wing. The crew was based at Long Binh Army Base, near Bien Hoa Army Base, a few miles northeast of Saigon.

"Spooky" gunship nose art
(Courtesy of Tyson V. Rininger)

The mission, piloted by Major Kenneth Carpenter, had been in the air for four-and-a-half hours, when the aircraft was hit by 82-mm mortar round (normally a ground-to-ground mortar) on the aft inboard right wing, leaving a three-foot hole and splintering shrapnel through the aft cargo area. They estimated that the attack left more than 3,500 holes in the airplane altogether.

The loadmaster, A1C [airman first class] John Levitow and Sergeant Ellis Owen had been preparing a Mark 24 magnesium flare (packed in a long tube and weighing about 27 pounds), when the first round hit the aircraft. Twenty-three-year-old Levitow had asked to fill in for the regular loadmaster on the mission; this was his 181st combat sortie. Levitow pulled Owens away from the open cargo door and spotted the flare, realized it was armed, and grabbed it, throwing it through the open door just before it ignited.[1] The flare would likely have burned through the floor and melted control cables for the rudder and elevator had it been left to ignite.

He accomplished this feat with more than 40 shrapnel wounds in his legs, side, and back. The sequence of events was later reconstructed by Carpenter using the smeared path of blood Levitow left on the floor of the compartment.

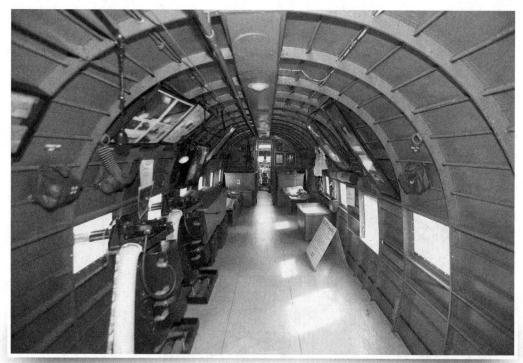

Spooky 71 interior
(Courtesy of Tyson V. Rininger)

The airplane made an emergency landing at Bien Hoa (aircraft home base), where Levitow aided in the evacuation of his crewmates before being ordered onto the med-evac aircraft himself. He was awarded the Medal of Honor for his selfless actions that night. He flew 20 additional combat missions after his recovery before returning to the U.S. to complete his enlistment as a C-141 loadmaster at Norton AFB in California. He passed away in 2000 after a long battle with cancer.[2]

The AC-47 proved that the airplane could evolve to fit roles that Douglas had never envisioned when first designing the DC-3. The airplane had the ability to withstand incredible amounts of damage, loiter for long periods of time at a relatively low airspeed on a given target, and carry a wide variety of crew and armament—making it a great answer to the military's needs in the Vietnam War.

1. U.S. Air Force Official Report; www.af.mil, accessed September 30, 2010
2. "The Amazing Gooney Bird: The Saga of the Legendary DC-3/C-47," by Carroll V. Glines

TOGETHER WE *Fly* VOICES FROM THE DC-3

He woke as if from a deep sleep, the grogginess that left him with the last dream. The smell of burnt rubber floated up around him, and the silver of twisted metal was the first thing he saw. The next, after blinking a few times and turning his head, was the broken windshield with the rain coming in, the drops quietly coursing down the glass, so different from the last of the pounding sheets they had entered at 11,000 feet over the San Ramons.

Before Willie could even turn to see the right seat and verify the truth with his eyes, he knew his co-pilot, Augustin, was dead. And he knew he was not, by the wetness of the air on his face, and the pain in his left leg where it was clamped between his seat and the control column. He closed his eyes again.

Just over the next hill, there was a small house made of stones painted burnt orange, with the chinking between a silty mustard, and an old woman sat on the steps looking out at the road. Girls in their school uniforms crossed ahead, looking barely aware of the random cars and trucks that would careen around the corner, no lines, no slowing for the inescapable human traffic walking along the tiny shoulders and in the road itself. Hydrangeas the color of faded light burst forth everywhere, coming through fences and holding up walls. Blue, but pale in the acidic soil that must contain the ashes from the volcano nearby. *Fresas frescas* bursting red in brown paper bags sold by the souvenir shops. Coffee green under its canopies, warming in the sun into the berries that still sold so well around the world.

Flowers and coffee, still the best exports from this small peaceful nation just six hours south of Dallas by the new jetprops. To get to those jets, some of the flower barons used trucks, but the roads were unpredictable, potholed in the rainy season and overflowing with people in the sun. Curving, twisting, climbing; taking an hour to cover 30 km. So the company's owner, Don Luis chose an airplane, the mighty DC-3, once used by LACSA and now supposed to be on its way to Panama after the stops in San Ramon and San Jose, Costa Rica. Willie and Augustin had left Tegu that morning. As he opened his eyes again, and looked around at the cockpit of the DC-3 contorted into a fun house, that morning seemed like someone else's memory.

Willie crawled out of the jungle bit up from the incessant attacks of hundreds of mosquitoes, no-see-ums, and see-um-all-too-wells. Two days later, only one of the bites gave him pause—instead of cresting and subsiding into a red pimple on his skin, this one just kept getting madder, redder, and more tender. One more reason in his mind that, in spite of the unforgiving hazards, it was better to fly above the hills than to hack one's way through them.

THE DC-3 AND C-47 SAW WIDESPREAD use throughout Central America from the 1950s through the 1980s, with a handful still in use in 2010. The region's remote airstrips and rudimentary maintenance facilities (in most areas) meant that the DC-3's performance and repairability in the field went a long way towards its success. Many ended up sold to Central American airlines and cargo operations, as well as to the various militaries in the region.

However, the lack of air traffic control and radar, weather reporting, and detailed maps conspired to create an environment where crews were on their own, and could get into dicey situations more readily than in other areas of operation. A handful of accident reports with no names and dangling entries in the aircraft registry illustrate this—and fuel the idea that there are airplanes out there waiting to be found.

A C-47B (construction number 14633, registration TI-1002) converted back to passenger configuration and operated by LACSA (Lineas Aereas Costarricenses, a Costa Rican airline) was one of these airplanes. On June 15, 1953, TI-1002 departed from Palmar Sur Airport (MRPM/PMZ) in southwestern Costa Rica—a small airport with a 3,183-foot airstrip. Its destination was San Isidro de el General airport (MRSI) in Costa Rica. The flight crashed into a hillside in the San Ramon Mountains in poor weather; all three crew perished, and six of the 12 passengers died as well. Perhaps

On the ramp at Guatemala City

DC-3s at Teguchigalpa, Honduras

all of its parts have been requisitioned for other uses, and others have become a part of the vegetation.

Another example: The fourth DST built, construction number 1497, began its life registered as NC16003 to American Airlines as the *Flagship Massachusetts*. It was converted to a C-49E model (USAAF number 42-56105) for World War II operations, then reverted back to civilian use. In 1949, it was sold to Rutas Aereas Mexicanas and operated as XA-HOS, where it may have fallen into paramilitary use. Its final disposition is not recorded, and where the fuselage ended up is unknown.

During visits to Guatemala, Honduras, Costa Rica, and Panama in the past five years, many DC-3s have been spotted in various states between operation and dereliction. An entire *fuerza aerea* waiting for deployment—just add parts, tools, commitment, and a lot of elbow grease.

The lights flickered on in the narrow street in Old Town San Juan, as Marta put the trash out into the alley. Her storefront was just six feet wide, but the location was good. She'd fought for it, putting together the money slowly to make the initial rent, then more quickly as her business picked up.

The sun was sinking below the ocean's rim, right on time, 6:30 p.m. The height of the hurricane season, but a clear night tonight, in advance of the next storm to march past them.

It was silly to her, but her best sellers, at least to the tourists, were not the bundled flower bouquets that she carried. Flags of Puerto Rico and magnets in the shape of the island, ironically, came in weekly from Miami, but the flowers came in every other day on a working-horse Four Star DC-3 from Charlotte Amalie. And the fruit...soursop, breadfruit, and star fruit, mostly. Her mouth watered thinking about it.

Earlier that afternoon, N135FS was quickly prepped for the 30-minute flight from STT to SJU, St. Thomas to San Juan, right on time, ready to depart at 1 p.m. A paint-splattered radio on the flatbed of a nearby pickup blasted the latest Madonna pop as the crew worked in the back of the airplane.

The mail went on board first, then the flats of bird-of-paradise flowers, orange points sticking up out of the buckets of water, shrouded in a fine netting to protect the fragile blooms. Other boxes, holding less fragile flowers, fruits, and trade goods fill the remaining space. It was nearly a full load, the copilot noted, but it was light, even with the buckets of water. She helped one of the linemen secure the last pallet before heading up front. The pilot closed the door and secured it from the inside after climbing on board.

The long, wide runway at Charlotte Amalie allowed for a low-key takeoff roll; without far to climb over the water for the trip, she kept the nose low and let the speed build past 115 knots as they passed over the end of the runway before giving a little more back pressure to the control wheel. A low layer of scattered puffy clouds laid shadows on the cerulean water, with random towers of white piercing the deck. A few little bumps played with the airplane as they passed through the cloud level.

She released the airplane from the climb at 3,000 feet msl, the sea shining and level as a pancake below. Just a short hop between islands, to be made as efficiently as possible. She smiled as she realized that she hadn't been above this altitude in months, it seemed.

The engines came back to cruise rpm and manifold pressure, 2050 and 25 inches respectively. The flowers would stay upright in their little nests in the back, and with the airflow through the open windows, the heat kept to a minimum. Can't have wilted flowers; they don't sell well in Old Town.

FOUR STAR AIRLINES WAS FOUNDED IN 1982 to serve the short-haul cargo needs of the Caribbean islands, primarily between Puerto Rico and the U.S. Virgin Islands. Runs to the Dominican Republic and other islands rounded out the company's schedule for almost 30 years. Four Star ceased operations in December 2009, a victim of inevitable change in economics, but the current management, led by Stuart Diamond, is working to return the DC-3s to service linking the islands.

"Business success in the Caribbean has little to do with any specialized management," said Arnaldo Gonzalez, long-time pilot for Four Star and other operations in the Caribbean. "It has more significantly to do with the regional ethnical understanding. The people around here believe that this is the center of the universe. Saint Thomas, Saint Croix and Beef Island are our preference [for transport operations] because [they are] in the profitable 150-mile radius. Beyond that, there is a chain of islands down to Trinidad and Barbados [that] belong either to the French, Dutch or British. The fuel cost is very expensive, and the islanders' business discipline is scarce, making it risky to operate down to the [se] islands. We do not need to go down [south] so far to make good business. A reliable operation to STT [St. Thomas, U.S. Virgin Islands] and STX [St. Croix, U.S. Virgin Islands] is enough.

Four Star DC3 *(Courtesy of Arnaldo Gonzalez)*

"We transport groceries, fruits, flowers, hardware, automobiles, boats, motorcycles and anything that fits inside the cabin with safety, which is our primary goal. The DC-3 still has and will have a place in air transportation, because it is the only one [that] has an endurance of seven hours in the air with a payload of 7,500 pounds covering a good profitable radius of 200 miles at a very comfortable cost," Gonzalez said in summary.

The DC-3 has been a standby in the islands and south Florida ever since its debut, and it remains the focus of stories fondly remembered by locals and visitors alike. Clay Greager from Last Flight Out, proprietor of the tourist shop in Key West (and a former Army helicopter pilot from the Vietnam era), related riding on one of three DC-3s that Air Sunshine operated between Key West and Miami from 1974 to 1979.

On one of the airplanes, the cockpit door latch was broken, so it would swing open during the flight. The flight lasted about an hour, to cover the 130-odd miles between Key West and Miami if you followed the string of keys. The flight attendant would roll out the cart, and then brace it sideways across the aisle at the front so that passengers could serve themselves during the flight.

"I remember drinking Welch's grape juice poured into a glass out of a number 10 can," said Greager. "Now how could I remember how many seats there were? I wasn't ever sober on those flights." That's because the last flight of the night left each evening at 11 p.m., more or less. Since the only transport off the island was by ferry or flight in those days, at the local bars the formal "Last call!" was replaced by "Last flight out!" to encourage folks to get on their way. Of course, if they weren't motivated enough, they might arrive at the airport to find that the last flight had already departed, leaving them to continue drowning their sorrows at the airport bar—not a bad place to cool one's heels, or so the story has it.

Baby Doll

S$3.75 per mile round-trip. Yep. That's it. No deals." The gruff man put the phone back in the cradle, its cord twirled into a series of wild figure 8s. He handed over a slip of paper to the pilot standing at the counter.

"Eight pallets. Into Metro. Have fun." The pilot looked at the slip but knew it would call for a pickup at Ft. Wayne, and a short leg over to Detroit and back that night. Easy one. The fuel load said it all: 600 gallons, the better half of it in the mains. Six hours. Enough for the round trip and an hour or two reserve. *Ah, it was a clear night,* he thought. *What could go wrong?*

The pilot helped the lineman load the pallets with the lift, watching in case one slipped and slid into the door jamb. Even though the old girl had taken her share of knocks, he knew just one of those 400-pound pallets could put the frame far enough out of square to prevent the door from closing, period. It was already tough to latch, with light from the ramp coming through a long gap along the bottom.

He ran off the aux tanks for the first 40 minutes, when the left engine fuel pressure started to fluctuate, then the 1830 coughed and died in a one-two punch. *I thought I had an hour and a half in there?* These old tanks leaked from time to time, so he chalked it up to that. But he figured he'd lost at least 70 gallons, if that was the case. Down to an hour reserve for sure. His supe would be torqued if he had to pick up fuel at Detroit—at least $5 a gallon, and at least twice as much as they paid at home base. *Ouch.*

He was more than halfway to Detroit, with the dark around him and below, the fields of southern Indiana, when he fell off into the half-light between awake and asleep. The copilot grew quiet, probably close to slumber himself. That's when he imagined the men who came before him, sitting in this seat, toughing out worse conditions than he'd ever see, short of being on fire. He had working radios, VOR, ADF, and air traffic control to talk to all the way, plus a transponder and radar to keep him separated from everyone else. He could look at the weather radar maps before he left, and talk with the folks at the flight service station to give him the big picture of the weather he'd confront on a given night. Those old pilots, those fellas flying this same airplane in the 1930s and '40s, they didn't have it so good as he did.

Same airplane, different era. He figured it would change again before his time was up. But it was hard to tell which era he was in during that dark, clear night, with only two-thirds of his panel properly illuminated by the instrument post lights. The rest was bathed in red, only a few shades off the sepia tone of a vintage movie.

EVEN THOUGH FLYING FREIGHT AT NIGHT in every weather condition imaginable is an experience some pilots gladly leave in the past, the pilots who flew the DC-3 generally look back with a fondness for the airplane that stood up to nearly every test. Terry Swindle was one of those pilots. "I flew for Academy Airlines [an air freight operation based in the Atlanta area in the 1970s, '80s, and '90s] from 1987 until 1991. N130D, N133D, and N143D were the backbone of the Academy fleet at the time. And flying the DC-3s was like a dream come true.

"With 969.6 hours in Academy DC-3s, I should have gotten a type rating. Shortly after I was hired at Academy, the company's designated examiner lost his medical, and nobody got type ratings while he was without one. He got it back shortly after I was hired at American Eagle."

Truitt Harper flew part of his career as a mechanic and freight pilot on the DC-3, and continues to crew on the airplane from time to time, as his admiration for the airplane only grows with time. Like other cargo operations, Academy's aircraft were converted with C-47 components, including landing gear and aft cargo doors, to better fit the mission of hauling as much as possible for as inexpensively as possible. He recalled his introduction to the airplane when he first began working for Academy.

"After returning from Africa as a pilot, I was looking for a flying job in Atlanta. I met a former friend who knew of a job flying cargo at night. I met with the owner, and he agreed to hire me as a mechanic and part-time copilot flying DC-3s. There were two of us in the training class, and following the second-in-command (SIC) training, we were to fly the routes together, one as the copilot, and the other, as observer, flying the jump seat. After a coin toss I was selected first to observe from the jump seat, and the other pilot would fly as second-in-command. On our very first trip, we had our introduction into the 'round engine experience.'

"We were to leave Des Moines, Iowa, with a load of cargo for Memphis, Tennessee, with an intermediate stop in Kansas City. It was early winter, 1977, so the weather was cold and icy. Following takeoff from Des Moines, as we climbed out, the captain pointed out that the oil temperature on one engine was rising, while the oil pressure was falling. Looking at the instruments, he said, 'If those two needles point at each other, we will have to feather the engine.' It was not very long until they were. The engine was feathered, and we asked for the weather at Des Moines. It was 300 overcast, three-quarter-mile visibility, winds 35 knots. The captain said, 'We are not doing a single-engine ILS approach into that type of weather.'

"We continued toward Kansas City with one engine feathered and the other engine at climb power. An hour-and-a-half later, we were in the clear and landing at Kansas City. Fortunately the wind was from the correct side to aid in our single-engine landing. After transferring the cargo to another aircraft I continued to Memphis, and the other two crew members remained with the broken airplane.

"The next trip that following day, I was in the right seat as second-in-command, since the other fellow said 'I can't deal with this,' and never showed up again for work! The aircraft that caused our exciting night was N143D."

"Several months into my flying career as a DC-3 captain, I experienced the following rather embarrassing situation [also in N143D]. We were en route from Memphis to New Orleans one early morning when one engine began to run very rough. After analyzing the situation, it was necessary to feather the engine. We were approximately 50 miles from New Orleans, and the weather was good.

"After an uneventful single-engine landing, the tower asked if I needed a tug to tow the plane into the ramp. As a still-green, macho captain, I said 'No, I'll just taxi in.' If you have ever tried to taxi a DC-3 with one engine feathered, you'll know why experienced captains would have requested a tow. Following many frustrating

N143D on night ramp at Thomaston, Georgia.
(Photo courtesy of Michael P. Collins, AOPA)

minutes of getting off the runway, onto the taxiway, and onto the ramp, we finally made it. I know the tower and other observers were entertained by the efforts of taxiing with one engine."

Other freight operations continued through the 1980s, 1990s, and through the present day. Rhoades Aviation, based in Columbus, Indiana, operated DC-3s converted with C-47 parts, and now operates a turbine conversion for short-haul charter trips. The money equation still makes sense for these aircraft; it's hard to find another airplane that can haul so much weight and bulk for as little operating expense.

Mitch Ellerbee recalls loading freight at Thomaston, Georgia, into a workhorse N143D in the 1990s. During the photo shoot for the image above, Ellerbee reminisced and said, "Now she's all prettied up like a baby doll."

Cold Ride

Time to put on the skis," he heard from behind the door. His dispatcher must be looking at the weather for tomorrow. Another night well below zero, the fifth night in a row, and here it was, only November. Up in the Northwest Territories, winter came early and stayed late. And the frozen lakes perfectly suited a ski-shod DC-3.

No matter. They took it as it came, the cold and the ice, the light and the dark. Thank goodness they had the option to fly.

After packing the cargo into the back, along with some dark green plastic lawn chairs—their use saw no season, he figured—the passengers came up the stair single-file for the short flight across the lake. Though the cold air blew in freely through the open double-wide cargo door, once they closed up the cabin would quickly warm from the body heat that radiated even through layers of coats and hats and scarves. Definitely the warm way to go, rather than a rough, six-hour ride through the vast plains.

The radials barked a bit in the chilly air, taking several rounds of the pre-oiler and a lot of coaxing before firing up. But once they started, they ran true. One flight down south this afternoon to Hay River, then back up the next morning. Every day they were just about full with passengers and their various baggage, like arctic commuters across a frozen land.

BUFFALO AIRWAYS USES ITS DC-3s STILL as part of a mixed fleet of freight and passenger-hauling airplanes throughout the Canadian North. The company began in 1970, and operates the DC-3s alongside the DC-4, Curtis C-46, Lockheed Electra L-188,

and more modern King Air, Cessna 185, Norseman, and Baron. "Buffalo Joe" McBryan founded Buffalo Airways, and still sits at the helm.

The Buffalo Airways DC-3s can be configured to haul up to 7,000 pounds of cargo and up to 27 passengers, depending on the need. Configured with C-47 cargo doors, and sometimes special ramps to load odd-sized and oversized equipment, the DC-3s could take on a handful of families or a dozen generators and other machines that would be otherwise hard to get to certain villages in the territory.

Scheduled flights still take place between Yellowknife (on the northern side of Great Slave Lake, in the Northwest Territories) and Hay River, on the south side. For roughly $200 one-way and $330 round-trip (less on weekends), you can take the 45-minute flight in relative warmth and comfort. The company's people believe that the airplane will still be used for many years to come, as there is no better replacement for it in their operations.

Buffalo Airways also uses its DC-3s to conduct pollution control and aerial survey, including geophysical survey and FLIR operations (using GPS and video imaging). Like any operation keeping the DC-3 flying, the company keeps a large inventory of spares on hand, along with experienced maintenance technicians wise to the ways of the airplane. Pilots still compete for jobs with the airline, beginning at the first rung of the ladder, sorting boxes with the company's courier service before moving into the right seat on the DC-3. When interviewed in 2005, Doug Veitch, then a longtime pilot and director for Buffalo Airways, related that the trip up the ladder wasn't for everyone, but if you made it, you felt like a real part of the company.

Once upon a time, Basler Airlines also used DC-3s to fly cargo and conduct charter operations in Canada from its home base in Wisconsin. Warren Basler appreciated the DC-3's payload, performance, and cubic volume, and in particular liked how it could get in and out of unpaved airstrips in the backcountry. But the engines? They showed their age, and were constantly threatening to break down while far from maintenance support.

Still, he could not come up with a good replacement for the DC-3. So he set out to improve the engines by installing the Pratt & Whitney PT-6A-67R turboprop engines and Hartzell five-blade props in place of the Twin Wasps with which the airplanes had been delivered. The first conversion was produced by Basler in 1982; certification as the BT-67 occurred in December 1990.

The complete conversion includes a total overhaul for the airframe and avionics as well as for the powerplants. The airplane

DC-3s undergoing conversion to BT-67 configuration at Basler

Interior modification to the BT-67 model at Basler

gets re-skinned with new aluminum and ribs, and fuel, hydraulic, and electrical systems are replaced with current-production
models. Upgrades specific to the customer's mission complete the
package.

The BT-67 has found customers all over the world. The
Columbian Air Force as well as the U.S. Forest Service have found
work for the airplane, which retails for a base price of $4.5 million
(in 2010). Drug-enforcement applications are popular, though it is
also used for troop transport, firefighting, and rainmaking.

As for running out of airframes, the company is not concerned;
they are still locating airframes ripe for refurbishment all over the
globe.

Idle Days

"The C-47 has no bugs. It has been around a long time doing a magnificent job. The only troubles you will have are those you bring on yourself."

—from *Pilot Training Manual for the Skytrain: C-47*, issued by the Army Air Force, August 15, 1945

He noticed when he studied the long list of Douglas production numbers that the DC-3s and the C-47s—along with the C-54s—were the aircraft that had strings attached, strings of registration numbers, conversion notes, and status updates. Few of the other models did. No one had much use for a B-17 after the war, but a C-47, well, that was a money-making machine right up through the present day. That's why the airplane that sat withering away in the grass down the field got under his skin.

DC-3 fans ("tourists," he called them) would come by from time to time, to scout around the pasty white hulk, bleached by so many summers sitting in the hot Southern sun. They'd snap a few pictures, post a story to a website, and then head out, some of them surely shaking their heads, as he did, as to the loss they felt. As we do with any airplane that is just left to corrode into nothing. That's just left to fade into the background.

He thought about putting the money together to bring it out of hibernation, but it always seemed that the hurdles were too high. Like any other classic airplane project, the money invested in bringing one back to life would never be recouped financially. Double that if you're dealing with big old radial engines. Nothing says "labor of love" like an aircraft restoration project. The only good reason to do it is because you have to: Something inside you just won't stop until you rescue that airplane.

A million dollars to do it right. And five years.

IF YOU LOOK AT THE LIST of production numbers for aircraft built by Douglas Aircraft Company, you see a theme amongst them all, and particularly amongst the DC-3s: the notation "WFU" or "W/O." These letters mean "withdrawn from use" and "written off" respectively, and they signify what you might think. The airplane has been totaled, whether from an accident or misuse or disuse, and nothing remains except perhaps a pile of parts or a data plate tucked in someone's desk drawer.

Sometimes, though, you'll see another set of letters: "DER." They mean "derelict," and indicate a sadder fate than that of airframes that went down in the heat of battle, or flying the line, or fulfilling their duty. These are the airplanes that have been left to rot. Left to commune with the weeds.

Ozark's N133D as the *Flagship Tennessee*
(Courtesy of C.R. Smith Museum and American Airlines, Inc.)

For example, here's the entry for one airplane:

"1936 DC-3A-S1C3G, c/n 1499, originally delivered as a DST, the *Flagship Tennessee*; last cert date 2002; DST-144 NC16005.

CONV. C-49E: 42-56092; then NC16005.

CONV. DC-3A: NC16005; then N16005; then N133D [DER]."

To translate this into plain English, the airplane is a 1936 DST-144, delivered on July 12, 1936, to American Airlines. It was converted as of May 28, 1942 into a C-49E for the United States Army Air Force, carrying USAAF serial number 42-56092. It was leased by American on April 22, 1943 to the Air Transport Command (ATC) and went in and out of service in the war. On March 21, 1945, it was returned to Douglas Aircraft Company as NC16005. On November 18, 1948, it transferred to an entity called WAA, and then was sold to Ozark in September 1950 as a re-commissioned DC-3A, as N133D and re-registered in 1957. It was returned to McDonnell–Douglas in December 1968 and sold to Airline Aviation Academy, in Griffin, Georgia, and

N133D sitting derelict
(Courtesy of Dan Gryder)

re-registered on May 26, 1970. It flew for a couple of decades, moving freight around the country. Now it sits, derelict.

Seven-hundred-and-fifty miles away, the folks at Tradewinds Aircraft Supply are making a living from parts piled up high on a lot next to San Antonio International Airport. Two DC-3 fuselages sit in the rear of the yard, with parts stacked neatly on open shelves nearby. Enough parts were produced during wartime for the DC-3 that the supply continues today, with outfits such as Tradewinds purchasing the treasure troves of these parts found in hangars and warehouses around the world. Many still bear the original Douglas factory tags. An entire machine shed's worth of more parts sits just a few yards away.

Inside that building, on a workbench, lays a massive tome, laid open like a Bible: the Douglas Illustrated Parts Catalog for the DC-3. It must be several hundred pages, covering every nut and

Tradewinds Aircraft
Supply lot

bolt on the airframe, with the thickness of each skin and the part
number for each Douglas-built component.

Many of those parts from
within the catalog lie within a
hundred feet of where it stands,
but one draws the eye: a pilot's
seat, all gussied up in primer
green and ready to go. That
sits by the open door, and the
sunlight shines in upon it. A
restoration seems possible,
even a grand idea, with such
a view.

Douglas Parts Catalog

Flying Again

The late May morning had started baking into place, the still air more of a hindrance than a help. He was about to start engines at the end of the grass runway at Gaston's White River Resort, in Lakeview, Arkansas. At least that wind wasn't blowing in the wrong direction. But Dan Gryder wasn't really worried. As he would say, "It doesn't even raise my blood pressure," but, if you knew him, you got the feeling he thought things through far more than he let on.

After the oil came up to temps and a quick run-up brought the engines into full rambling mode, he lined up the airplane, straightening the tailwheel to lock it into place. Holding the brakes, he brought the engines up to 25 inches, then 30, then more. Releasing the brakes, and the DC-3 rolled down the grass downriver. In just a hundred feet, the tail came up, flying. Now it would take nearly 2,800 feet more to bring the rest of the airplane up off the ground into ground effect, finally, and then into a gentle climb. But he planned it that way, knowing speed is your friend, and altitude only a false comfort.

As he turned to the right to cut behind the trees at the end of the runway, following the contours of the hayfield beyond, there was an appreciable intake of breath among those visiting the resort who had come out to watch. They couldn't see him climb out over the river valley, but the golden moment of silence that followed his departure said it all.

What a glory to behold, a classic airplane doing what it ought to do: Fly.

GRYDER NETWORKS BOUGHT N143D from Academy Airlines in 2001. After decades as primarily a cargo-hauling workhorse, the airplane took well to its new role, now almost exclusively a training airplane. Dan Gryder named the airplane *Darla Dee* after his wife to show his thanks for her support.

With the purchase of the airplane, Gryder secured a handful of training contracts, including the initial and recurrent training contract for FAA pilots operating N34, the historic flight inspection DC-3. He also began marketing the airplane to pilots around the world who had always dreamed of flying the airplane, and maybe getting a pilot-in-command or second-in-command type rating in it to show proudly on a pilot certificate. A few sought to purchase DC-3s of their own, and needed the type rating to see that through. Only a small handful of DC-3s have operated as training airplanes after 2000, and N143D remains as one of those few.

The airplane had undergone significant changes since its Ozark days, with several C-47-based conversions made to the airframe to allow it to operate at a higher maximum gross weight of 26,900 pounds and carry more cargo. Gryder returned N143D to a Part 91 operating certificate, which limited the maximum gross takeoff weight to 25,200 pounds. Most training flights, in fact, dispatch at 21,000 to 23,000 pounds with fuel, equipment, and aspiring DC-3 pilots on board.

At the same time, Gryder sought out opportunities to demonstrate and display the airplane at various airshows, determined to put the legendary airplane in front of modern audiences. One of their first major outings was participation in the Centennial of Flight celebration at Kill Devil Hills, North Carolina, in 2003. In 2005, the airplane became sponsored in part by Herpa Miniature Models, and covered with a design scheme to match a run of high-quality die-cast models produced by the German company. In this configuration, N143D made performances at Sun 'n' Fun Fly-In in

Takeoff at Gaston's White River Resort

Bee Haydu, WASP, at the controls of N143D, en route to Oshkosh in July 2010.
(Courtesy of Dan Gryder)

Lakeland, Florida, in 2006 and 2007, as well as at regional shows across the southeastern United States. Two long cross-country trips in the airplane during the summers of 2008 and 2009 took the airplane each time on a two-week road show into small airports and communities around the Midwest.

Most fulfilling to Gryder has been sharing the airplane with people from all walks of life who come out to see it. Maybe because they attach a powerful memory to the airplane, or maybe because it just takes up so much ramp space wherever it goes—the airplane attracts people to it like few others on the circuit. To give a veteran the opportunity to show his grandchild the airplane he flew in the war, or a WASP a chance to sit left seat in the airplane she ferried—those are the moments he treasures.

Gryder shares a story that illustrates this vividly. "Quite a while ago, an older gentleman called and reserved a one-hour flight in our DC-3. At 73 years old, he had enjoyed a long and impressive career in aviation. His hands and his pilot certificate were equally well worn, and I wondered how many landings those hands had been through. But he wanted to fly the DC-3, and that is the only reason he was there. So together, we flew. Although this was his first time in the left seat of any DC-3, he handled the craft with smoothness and finesse, like this flight was one that he had thought a lot about.

"Back on the ground and sitting at our table, we talked some more and he produced a thick black logbook, and asked for my signature. The black book was also worn like his hands, but he had all of his totals accurately counted up, representing a lot of flight time, and a lot of history I am sure. I signed the entry line with the date, the N number, and the aircraft type: DOUGLAS DC-3. When I was done writing, he took the book back. With a black pen, he drew one diagonal black line through all the remaining entry lines on the page. Then I watched as he wrote the word 'END' in big letters. He closed the logbook and wrapped a rubber band around it, then shook my hand.

"It was just dawning on me what this DC-3 flight had been about for him. He thanked me for helping him end his flying career by fulfilling a lifelong dream, a dream of flying the DC-3. 'I'm all done, it's been a great ride, and I wouldn't change any of it. But it's too hard to keep my medical now, my vision isn't what it was, and there's just no point. There is no better way to end my aviation career than with this flight,' he said."

In April 2005, N143D suffered a gear collapse while Gryder conducted training in it at Thomaston, Georgia. The drag strut linkage on the right main landing gear had failed catastrophically just as the airplane was rolling to a stop after a normal landing. As the gear collapsed, the strut punched up through the top of the wing behind the engine nacelle and folded the gear beneath it, causing the prop to strike the asphalt, and the wingtip to scrape a runway light as the airplane pitched to the right and forward.

The resulting damage to the airplane looked catastrophic as well, at first, but there was no one hurt, and no fire. And amazingly, the incident led Gryder to understand and appreciate the Douglas engineering team even more than he had before. Because of the way the airplane was designed, the collapse did not rupture a single fuel line or tank, nor did it harm the carry-through spar caps in the wing. Though returning the airplane to flight took five months, the process served as a great teacher, unveiling by chapters the decisions made by Douglas as the original blueprints were drawn nearly 70 years before.

For example, the wing skin of the DC-3 is actually constructed of two sheets of aluminum: one is the smooth layer you see on the outside, but this is riveted under compression to a corrugated

Right: The drag strut punched up through the wing.

Below: The wing repair, showing the corrugation under the smooth top skin.

layer underneath. The result is a much stronger load-carrying structure. The wing spar consists of the spar caps, which are attach angles that run through the center section of the airplane, and also spar web—sheets of aluminum that butt up against each other, transferring load like a continuous spar, yet far more repairable in the field and at less cost.

Members of the DC-3 community showed support throughout the repair process by helping Gryder source parts (many with those original Douglas stickers still affixed) and understand various techniques required to get the job done. By September 2005, N143D was flying again, and she was featured in the December 2005 issue of *AOPA Pilot* magazine. More importantly, a feeling of kinship with the airplane took root, one that would lead Gryder to envision an appropriate celebration for the airplane's 75th anniversary in 2010.

First you heard the sound of the pre-oiler humming on a lone engine, driving oil into the cylinders for a healthy start. Then you saw the blades turn on that single engine: one... two... three... then eleven blades come to top center. Then the click of the ignition, introduction of full rich mixture, and a little throttle. More blades. Then the engine caught, and sent a cough or two of smoke out as it rumbled to life.

Repeat that sequence 52 times within a 5-minute period. Then imagine the sound as you stand there on the ramp, the roar all around you. The smell of oil burning and cut grass and hot cement. Fifty-two Pratt & Whitney 1830s starting one after the other. Fifty-two *successful* engine starts, from engines that have been around for seven *decades*. Almost a statistical impossibility, yet on that beautiful July afternoon, history was made before the pack of DC-3s and C-47s even left the ground. You could feel it as much as see it.

After starting up, the lead aircraft, N143D, taxied out to the runway as briefed, followed by the next two DC-3s to be ready in sequence. The briefing that morning had covered every contingency, and set forth a plan that would get the airplanes into the formation as smoothly and efficiently as possible, giving a nod to the fact that at least one would be expected to abort from the mission on takeoff, based on percentages alone.

Twenty-six airplanes followed the first one out to the runway, and for the next 15 minutes, a DC-3 or C-47 took off from Whiteside County Airport about once every 30 to 45 seconds. After takeoff, the lead aircraft in each three-ship element followed a large rectangular track to the east, then south, then west to allow for the element to assemble. Three airplanes taxied back in; two having planned to do so, and one truly aborted its takeoff because of an engine concern. A crowd watched from the flight line, and a small group of photographers stood out by the wind circle, waiting for the twenty-three airborne planes to return.

The parade caused time to stand still. You could imagine, looking up as each trio thundered overhead, how it would have felt to witness a similar stream of airplanes rolling past 65 years ago, as part of the war effort. Or how it would have felt to be on the busy ramp at New York with a dozen DC-3s starting engines and taxiing past to keep the airline's schedule.

One thing was for certain: No one there at Rock Falls would ever forget the sight and the sound and the feeling. The only experience more awe-inspiring? To be on board a DC-3 taking off from Santa Monica on a December afternoon later that year, 75 years after the eve of its first flight.

∼

The Last Time

TWENTY-SEVEN AIRPLANES HAD GATHERED AT ROCK Falls, Illinois, at the Whiteside County Airport, for "The Last Time," a reunion for DC-3s, their pilots, and crews, and enthusiasts from around the world. One of the two DC-2s still flying also joined the event, which ran from July 24 to July 26, 2010.

Twenty-three of the airplanes participated in a mass formation flight to honor Douglas and his legacy, and 21 flew in that formation from Rock Falls to Oshkosh, Wisconsin, for the AirVenture fly-in. The people of Rock Falls and Sterling (the town next door) rolled out the red carpet for the crews and fans of the DC-3, and ensured that every arrangement was made and every logistical challenge was anticipated.

Trevor Morson has been the tireless webmaster for the Douglas DC-3 historical website, "The DC-3 Hangar" (www.douglasdc3.com) since 2000, and the site reflects the wide variety of information and stories that people continue to share about the airplane and their relationships to it. So it was only fitting that Morson was there for the 75th anniversary event. "I am lucky to live in Aurora, Illinois," said Morson. "Whiteside Airport in Rock Falls is only an hour drive west for me and 'The Last Time' was to be the largest gathering of DC-3s. With media credentials and VIP tickets in hand, my girlfriend Patti and I were very excited to be a part of this event over the next three days.

"Just a mile or so out before arrival, we were blessed to see a C-47 in World War II Normandy markings fly right across us at only a few hundred feet above the I-88 highway. With the sound of those humming Pratt & Whitney engines, this was truly our own personal welcome and the rush of adrenalin it provided marked our arrival much like a salute in a perfect way. It was a sight to behold and it will be an everlasting memory for me.

"We first checked into our hotel a few minutes away from the airport, and it was evident that the entire community were supportive and excited to be part of this historic celebration. With everybody wearing DC-3 t-shirts, and signs, flyers, and billboards with 'Welcome DC-3 enthusiasts' everywhere, along with a couple of DC-3s now flying over us in formation, we quickly realized that we had just arrived into 'DC-3 Heaven!'

Ramp at The Last Time *(Courtesy of Trevor Morson)*

"Our arrival at Whiteside airport on the morning of Saturday, July 24, 2010, was no disappointment. We could see many DC-3s parked everywhere and it was 'all access.' Our first chore of the day was to find Dan Gryder, chief pilot of the Herpa DC-3, N143D. I had worked with Dan through email about this event, and I have actually known Dan for many years via the Internet. This was to be our first-ever face to face meeting. Surprisingly, Dan was easy to find, and though he was very busy as the main organizer of this event, we found the time to greet each other, shake hands and chat for a while.

"Throughout the next three days we embraced the sights and sounds of 26 DC-3s and a DC-2. We spoke with many DC-3 pilots — some I have known for a long time — and it was good to catch up on the DC-3 news past and present. We would gather in the VIP hangar sharing stories and discuss DC-3 topics such as the 'de-rated power takeoff.' (Yes, this controversial DC-3 discussion still exists between us all: Do you use 44 inches of manifold pressure on takeoff? 46

Watching the takeoff parade at The Last Time

inches? Or full power at 48 inches?) This was a fun topic, and we often laughed about it. Steve Dunn, pilot of the Eastern Airlines DC-3, N18121, used 52 inches of manifold pressure (because his airplane has the Pratt & Whitney R1830-94 DC-3 engines).

"I have always found it interesting how music and aviation seem to go hand in hand. The band '100 Obscured' entertained us in the VIP hangar and then late into the moonlit evening sitting under a DC-3, playing songs by request. Being a musician myself, I had the chance to jam on the guitar with the band, and it provided a perfect ending each night to three perfect days of experiencing this historic event.

"The second day, more DC-3s arrived, and it was the perfect day for me to have my friend Jim take me up in his Mooney for some of the best aerial photography shots one could ever take. It would be the only way you get each of the 26 DC-3s (and a DC-2) in one photograph.

"The third and final day, Monday, July 26, all of the DC-3s were to take off and fly in formation heading north to EAA's Oshkosh airshow. This was a fantastic sight to see and made for another everlasting memory for all those thousands of people who attended the event, volunteers, supporters and enthusiasts alike. We all just witnessed history before our very eyes. 'The Last Time' event was indeed 'DC-3 Heaven,' but I am hopeful this is 'The First Time' of many more DC-3 gatherings to come."

Airport manager Mike Dowell led the team that coordinated efforts to park and service every airplane and take care of everyone,

Formation flight at The Last Time
(Courtesy of Greg Morehead)

using the wide ramp and closing north-south runway to handle the folks who flew in to visit. The Last Time organizers were ready with spare parts, tools, ladders, drums of oil, and personnel to take care of any maintenance item that cropped up, but in the end, they hardly needed to do so much as put air in a tire. All of the aircraft came in ready to fly, and fortune shined on the event.

The DC-3, like many other historic aircraft, faces a confluence of looming hazards that conspire to take it out of the skies. Most DC-3 pilots and owners agree that we have the talent and resources to keep the airplanes flying for as long as there is a will to do so. But uncertainties exist surrounding the future of aviation fuel compatible with the big radial engines, and the creep of bureaucracy and superfluous regulations threaten to make it ever more of an uphill battle to keep these precious pieces of history—and modern creativity—flying. For one weekend in July 2010, all of those concerns were set aside for the celebration, even if it would be the last time so many would gather.

75th Anniversary

ON A SUNNY AND COLD DECEMBER afternoon at the Santa
Monica Airport, a group of friends gathered to make a very special
flight. No fanfare, no eloquent speeches, no buzz—just a routine
flight to capture photos of the airplane on the eve of its 75th anniversary. The next day, December 17, the true anniversary, would
be dreary and wet, with low ceilings and visibility precluding a
recreation of the first flight. On that day, we would join Douglas
Aircraft Company colleagues and retirees to mark that milestone
at Long Beach, and share stories with the people whose lives inter-
twined with that of the airplane.

With the conditions on December 16, 2010, at Santa Monica
closely matching those of December 17, 1935, and the sun sinking
down towards the Pacific Ocean, we (being realists like Douglas
himself) felt certain this was the best way to capture the spirit of
that world-changing flight. We stopped by the site of the Douglas
factory on Wilshire Boulevard on our way to the airport, and saw
N47SJ, the DC-3C/C-47 we would fly, joining the downwind, making a beautiful sound as it cut through the soft blue sky.

On the ramp at Atlantic Aviation, we restarted the engines on
a spot of ground that had been part of the original Douglas factory at Santa Monica, on Ocean Park Boulevard. As we taxied out,

everyone stopped to watch our stately progression to the north-east end of the field. The airport is now one of the most heavily restricted in the western U.S., pummeled with noise abatement warnings and a surrounding public that doesn't always recognize the importance of their airport neighbor. To us, the sound of the Pratts, low and steady, created music and a ripple of energy that flowed back through the fuselage as pilots Sherman Smoot and Dan Gryder completed the run-up. Just like Cover and Collbohm nearly 75 years ago, the pilots knew the oil had to come up to temperature, and preflight checks had to be satisfactory before they would consider a takeoff.

The runway now points to a heading of 210, rather than more westerly (as it did in 1935), but the spot where we started rolling was as close to that of the original takeoff roll as possible. We levitated into the air, easy on the engines, and gaining altitude at a steady rate over town as we headed towards the ocean. The pilots shaded their eyes from the sun as it bounced off the water in a starburst, and we turned north over the beach, passing over the Santa Monica Pier.

During an hour of slow circles in the sky, we all reflected in our own ways about the significance of the airplane. On the first flight, Cover and Collbohm followed procedures within a careful envelope, testing systematically a list of items, much as we do today during a first flight. They were both engineers and pilots, collecting the data to take back to the engineers on the ground so that inevitable adjustments could be made.

On the anniversary flight

Looking out of the windows, the passengers looked out at the Malibu hills and the beaches filled with people enjoying the afternoon, with those flying on the opposite end of the telescope from those on the ground. It must be that on the ground you are looking backwards through the telescope, your world so small in comparison to the view from the sky.

From this point, with enough fuel, we could fly to Hawaii, and that airplane made it possible to connect people and places like never before. Wars would be fought and won with the airplane, and lives saved both in its ability to deliver critical supplies and rescue refugees from horrific fate.

But more than anything, I thought of Donald Douglas. While he would push Douglas Aircraft Company into the jet age and into space, the DC-3 synthesized for the first time every element required to bring commercial success to aviation. His work up to that point had been in creating the foundation—in the engineering and in the company—that could support the DC-3's design. There was a reason he took the calculated risk to stretch and improve the DC-2 and answer that call. And just as I feel he was watching in private that first flight 75 years ago, he was somewhere close on its anniversary, watching, satisfied, as we flew to celebrate his airplane, the airplane that changed the world.

All quotes from Trevor Morson are from the author interview.

THERE'S NO MORE FITTING TRIBUTE TO the DC-3 and their creator than the fact that so many remain airworthy through the airplane's 75th anniversary year. The DC-3 continues on, flying on a strength greater than the sum of its parts.

The following is a roll call of Douglas Aircraft Company airplanes participating in "The Last Time" event, July 2010, in reverse chronological order, by Douglas construction number.

N3006: 1946 DC-3; c/n 42961; *Esther Mae.* Built in 1946, this aircraft is one of the youngest of the type flying. She has been a corporate aircraft her entire life. Built under a U.S. Air Force contract as a C-117 at the very end of World War II, she was converted to a DC-3 at the Douglas Santa Monica factory and sold into civilian use when all government contracts were cancelled. *Esther Mae* is still operated today as a corporate aircraft and flies under 14 CFR Part 135 regulations. She's based in Aurora, Oregon, and owned by DC-3 Entertainment.

N1944H: 1944 DC-3; c/n 34378; *The Spirit of Alaska.* Originally owned by the United States Army, the DC-3 started its life in 1945 as 45-1108, a C-47B. She was then delivered to the United States Air Force. In March 1946, she was put in the care of the RFC, Reconstruction Finance Corporation. With only 35.5 hours, she was flown to Mineola, New York, and sold to a gentleman who wanted to start an airline. In early 1946, she was converted to an executive DC-3 by Aero Trades, Inc., as NC54542, and she became the corporate aircraft for the Columbia Broadcasting System (CBS). She was sold in 1948 and flew as N280M for Outboard and Marine Manufacturing Company (OMC) from December 1966 to

March 1977. OMC then donated the DC-3 to the Experimental Aircraft Association (EAA). During this time, she was re-registered as N54542. EAA later sold her to California Air Tours. In April 1995, Era Classic Airlines purchased the aircraft and renamed her *The Spirit of Alaska*, and gave nostalgic air tours. In 2003, she was sold and currently resides in Rockford, Illinois, with about 17,700 hours.

N97H: 1945 DC-3; c/n 33613. In 1945 she was delivered to the U.S. Army as 44-77281 as a C-47B. In 1948, she was sold to Humble Oil and Refining Company, in Houston, Texas. In 1967, she went to William H. Wheeler of Tyler, Texas, and, in 1979, to Bill Bob Barnett, of Billy Bob's Texas Night Club, in Fort Worth, Texas. In 1983 she went to AFS Leasing for a charter service called "Sentimental Journeys," operated out of Bluefield, West Virginia. In 1988, Otis Spunkmeyer Cookie Company, of San Leandro, California, purchased the airplane. In 1999, she was sold to Bud Field Aviation, in Hayward, California. In 2004, she was purchased by Steve Hiller, Hiller Aviation Museum, in San Carlos, California. 97H was the sister ship to Jim Gabbert's N41HQ when the Otis Spunkmeyer Cookie Company owned them and gave tours around the San Francisco Bay area. Many people have been married on these two aircraft while flying over the Golden Gate Bridge.

N34: 1945 DC-3; c/n 33359. N34, the FAA's last DC-3, was completed in May 1945 by the Douglas Aircraft Company plant in Oklahoma City, in what is now building 3001 at Tinker Air Force Base. It was finished as a U.S. Army Air Force TC-47B as 44-77027, but re-assigned to the United States Navy as an R4D-7 navigation trainer (Bureau No 99856) and later converted to an RD4-6R. It served in various transport squadrons at Norfolk, Virginia; Quonset Point, Rhode Island; London, England; and NAS Glenview, Illinois, until 1956. In 1958 it was loaned to the CAA (the predecessor of the FAA), where it was converted to a flight inspection aircraft. In 1966, the aircraft became FAA property, was upgraded to its current configuration, and continued as a flight inspection aircraft, one of 60 such FAA DC-3s, until 1979, mostly operating out of California. N34 ended its career as the main flight inspection training aircraft in Oklahoma City in 1980 and 1981. In 1985 it was taken out of storage, repainted in the CAA 1955 vintage colors, and operated as a recruiting and information tool at airshows until it was placed in storage again in 1995. N34 was reconditioned for a third life in 2002 to participate in the U.S. National Centennial of Flight in 2003, and it celebrated the Oklahoma State Centennial in 2007. In 2008, it celebrated the 50th Anniversary of the creation of the FAA. N34 is one of two items on the National Register of Historic Places that moves (the other being the Cable Cars of San Francisco), placed on the register on May 29, 1997. N34 is based at Oklahoma City.

N8704: 1944 DC-3; c/n 33048; *Yankee Doodle Dandy.* She was manufactured by Douglas Aircraft in Oklahoma City, and delivered to the U.S. Army Air Force on April 11, 1945. Her assignments were in Texas, California, and Arizona, and she was on loan to the University of Michigan from Selfridge Air National Guard Base until August 1970. After her work with the Environmental Research Institute of Michigan was concluded, the Yankee Air Museum purchased the aircraft and restored her completely inside and out. After restoration in 1985, she was awarded the "Best of Transport" citation at Oshkosh, Wisconsin. She is owned by Yankee Air Museum, and based at Willow Run Airport, Detroit, Michigan.

N25641: 1943 DC-3; c/n 32883. She began life as a C-47-DL, delivered to the U.S. Army Air Force as 42-32833. She came off the line on February 11, 1943, and was delivered to Oran, Algeria, on August 17, 1943. She saw action in the Mediterranean and European theaters, and was there for the D-Day invasion when squadrons of DC-3s towed gliders laden with combat soldiers into battle. Work orders for the "repair of bullet holes" are still among her logs. She was transferred to the 8th Air Force and arrived back in the United States on August 17, 1945. At the conclusion of the war, she was sold into private hands and upgraded from military freighter to executive aircraft. She flew out of Shreveport, Louisiana for nearly 25 years. Another 25 years and five owners later, she was purchased by Erik L. Fleming, President of Fleming Corporation. She went through a major restoration, with 14 passenger seats, and now serves as Legend Airways' lead aircraft.

N47SJ: 1944 C-47B; c/n 25869; *Betsy's Biscuit Bomber.* She was built in the Douglas factory at Tulsa, Oklahoma, and delivered to the U.S. Army Air Force as 43-48608. She saw deployment in the European theater in World War II, primarily in Belgium and France. She was based in Israel for more than 30 years following the war, and then went to Canada. Currently owned by the Gooney Bird Group and piloted by Sherman Smoot, she still has her original interior, and is based in Paso Robles, California. She has accumulated roughly 9,400 hours, and flew the 75th anniversary flight on December 16, 2010, from Santa Monica Airport in California.

N2805J: 1944 AC-47; c/n 20835; *Spooky 71.* She was delivered as a C-47B-1-DL to the U.S. Army Air Force as 43-16369, then registered as N2805J, and repurposed as an AC-47 gunship for the Vietnam War as 43-770. She was then re-registered as N2805J following her return to the United States. She was restored to emulate the Spooky gunship flown by Major Carpenter and crewed by John Levitow during the incident in which Levitow earned his Medal of Honor. She is currently owned by the American Flight Museum and based in Topeka, Kansas.

N47060: 1943 C-47A-65-DL; c/n 19066. She was delivered in 1943 to the U.S. Army Air Force as 42-100603. Later, she was designated an R4D-5 and delivered to the U.S. Navy as number 39095. She returned to Air Force service as 43-9095, and was subsequently re-registered as N47060. Her current owner is the Northern Illinois Aircraft Museum.

N3239T: 1943 C-47A; c/n 19054; *Tico Belle.* She was built in 1942 and delivered in 1943 to the U.S. Army Air Force as 42-100591. She departed for England in 1944, and upon arrival was assigned to the 9th Army Air Force. She was further assigned to the 437th Troop Carrier Group (TCG) and the 84th Troop Carrier Squadron (TCS), joining others at RAF Ramsbury. She was in position number 50 during the 437th's first operation in the Normandy invasion, towing a Waco CG-4 troop-carrying glider. She supported further campaigns in Western Europe through the war, including the Battle of the Bulge, resupplying the village of Bastogne. She returned to Indiana in August 1945. She was called out of storage to assist in the Berlin Airlift, from 1948 to 1949. In 1950, the Norwegian Air Force took delivery of her as part of the Lend-Lease program. In 1956, she was transferred to the Royal Danish Air Force, where her duty assignment was to transport the Royal Family of Denmark. In 1982 with over 13,500 flying hours, the Royal Danish Air Force finally retired her. Valiant Air Command, based in Titusville, Florida, purchased her to support airshows and other events.

N47E: 1943 C-47; c/n 13816. Built as a C-47A in Long Beach California, she rolled off the assembly line on September 23, 1943. She was delivered to the U.S. Army Air Force as 43-30665. She operated at various stateside locations during the 1940s, 1950s and

1960s. From 1966 to 1972, she operated at the U.S. Army Proving Grounds at Ft. Huachuca, Arizona. In May 1975, she was sold as surplus to Summer Institute of Linguistics, in Waxhaw, North Carolina, where she operated in South America under the registration of HK-2540P. In April 1990, she was purchased by her current owner, K&K Aircraft/Dynamic Aviation.

N353MM: 1943 C-53; c/n 11665. She was built as a C-53D-DO and delivered to the U.S. Army Air Force as 42-68738. She was converted to a DC-3A configuration following the war and carried the N66W registration. The airplane is now a freshly restored C-53 paratrooper plane to reflect her D-Day history. Her current configuration is as a deluxe family airliner with 19 seats.

N59NA: 1943 C-47; c/n 9043. This Douglas C-47-DL is the oldest surviving ex-RAF Dakota transport. On February 13, 1943, she was completed at Long Beach, California, factory as 42-32817. On March 7, 1943, she was delivered to Royal Air Force as FD789 (Dakota MK. I) under the Lend-Lease arrangement. From April 10, 1943, to April 17, 1946, she was used in a variety of roles throughout Great Britain. Then she was ferried to No. 22 MU (Maintenance Unit) at FAF Silloth, Northumberland, Cumbria, England, for storage. This airfield was used after the war for storage and scrapping of Ansons, Dakotas, Lancasters, Yorks and other aircraft. On November 28, 1947, she was registered as G-AKNB with Scottish Aviation in Preswick, Scotland, and on August 19, 1948, to Guinea Air Traders. On February 14, 1950, she was sold to Field Aircraft Services and flown to Burma, and registered as XY-CAN with Union of Burma Airways. On October 19, 1950, she was sold to British European Airways, registered as G-AKNB, and nicknamed "Sir Sefton Brancker." On December 11, 1959, she was sold to Silver City Airways and named "City of Bradford." On January 23, 1962, she was sold to British United Airways and operated mostly in the Channel Islands through 1968. She was featured in the movie, "The Eagle Has Landed," in 1976. On October 13, 1978, she was sold to Mercantile Aviation, in Ireland, operating as Clyden Airways, and registered as EI-BDU. In January 29, 1982, she was sold to Aces High, Ltd. registered as G-AKNB and based in Duxford, Cambridgeshire, England, from January 1982 through August 1985. She was painted as FD 789 for the movie "The Dirty Dozen," and placed on display at the Imperial War Museum collection at Duxford, Cambridgeshire, England. She also took part in the film "War and Remembrance." She was sold to Northern Airways, flown to Burlington, Vermont, and registered as N459NA.

After several owners in the U.S., she was sold in October 2007 to BGA Aviation, Inc. of Bennettsville, South Carolina, her current owner.

N5106X: 1943 C-47-DL; c/n 9058. She was delivered to the U.S. Army Air Force as 42-32832, and she flew with the 53rd Troop Carrier Squadron, successfully dropping 18 paratroopers on June 6, 1944, during the D-Day invasion, with no casualties. 42-32832 is the only surviving C-47 from the original 13 that formed the 53rd Troop Carrier Squadron. Following the war, she returned to the U.S., was re-registered as NC75412 and converted to a DC-3C by the Executive Transport Corporation. After conversion the aircraft was sold to General Motors, Inc., in Detroit, Michigan, where it was assigned a new registration number, N5106. In May 1967, she was re-registered N5106X, and during November 1967, she was donated to the Board of Trustees, Southern Illinois University, at Carbondale, Illinois, which converted her to a 24-passenger configuration. The aircraft was sold to Henry Oliver III in July 1985. Oliver sold it to Bygon Aviation, where she was flown on a Part 135 certificate for a short period of time. She was then sold to the David Nickolas, of Organ Donor Awareness Foundation, Inc., and operated by heart transplant recipient Rodney DeBaun. Scott Glover bought the airplane on August 4, 2000.

N92578: 1943 C-47-DL; c/n 9028. She was delivered to the U.S. Army Air Force as 42-32802 in 1943, and was re-registered for commercial service as NC9562H in 1946, then again as N13875 for National Automotive Fibres, Inc. of Detroit, Michigan, in 1953. She was registered as N75C for the Detroit Steel Corp in 1966. Next, she was re-registered as N7503 to Ohio University, in Athens, Ohio, in 1968, which was changed to N1800U in October 1969. She changed registration again to N1800D. Her next owner was Jungle Aviation & Radio Service, who took ownership in November 1971, based in Waxhaw, North Carolina. In 1973, she went to South America as CP-1020 for the Instituto Linguistico de Verano. She was registered again as N92578 in August 1981. She took her present registration numbers for California Air Tours, in California, in August 1989. In 1990, she went to Nostalgia Air Tours in Hawaii. Next, she was registered to DC-3 Inc. in Nantucket, Maine, in June 1991. During the 1990s, she was completely overhauled by the Santa Barbara Aerospace Company at San Bernardino Airport in California. She is currently owned by Airborne Imaging of Houston, Texas.

N87745: 1941 C-49J; c/n 6315; *Southern Cross*. She was delivered to the U.S. Army Air Force in November 1941. She was given to Delta Airlines in March 1942, and then to Continental Airlines. She was then converted to a DC-3 in 1944 and used by the Department of Transportation into the 1970s. During that time, the engines were converted to the Wright Cyclone 1820-76D, making her one of the very few flying with 1,475 horsepower on each wing. She then went to Mexico in 1976, and came back to the U.S. and Southern Cross Airways in the 1980s as a jump plane. Five jumpers have died who jumped out of Southern Cross. She is currently owned by Terry Patrick and based at Fort Worth's Meacham Field.

N737H: 1942 C-47-DL; c/n 6062. She was delivered to the U.S. Army Air Force as 43-30631, and then designated as an R4D-1 and given to the U.S. Navy as 12396. Following the war, she was converted to a DC-3C and registered as NC39340. Over the years, she was re-registered as N69011, then N7H, and finally as N737H.

N1XP: (not in formation) 1942 C-47-DL; c/n 4733; *Duggy*. The airplane was delivered to the U.S. Army Air Force as 41-38630 in 1942. Other registrations include VHC-DR; VHC-FV, NC843, N843K, CF-DOT, and C-FDOT. During its history, it was converted to a DC-3. Currently owned by Duggy Foundation, it is based at Fargo Air Museum at Hector International in Fargo, North Dakota, and used for youth outreach and other civic programs.

N44V: 1942 DC-3; c/n 4545. The Carolinas Aviation Museums Piedmont DC-3 was built for the U.S. Army Air Force in 1942 as a C-47. It served exclusively in the United States during World War II. After the war it served in a number of civilian roles in both the U.S. and Canada. During this period it underwent several upgrades including the replacement of the original cargo door with the air-stair. Piedmont acquired the aircraft in 1986 to 1987, but never flew this aircraft in airline service. After its retrofit into Piedmont colors, Piedmont, and then USAir, flew this aircraft as a flying museum and as a corporate relations aircraft until 1996. The aircraft was then purchased from USAir by the Carolinas Aviation Museum with the assistance of many sponsors, including many ex-Piedmont Airlines employees. It is based at Charlotte, North Carolina, and has approximately 15,700 airframe hours.

N150D: 1941 C-47; c/n 4463; *Judy*. She rolled off of the Douglas production line on November 18, 1941, in Santa Monica and delivered on June 23, 1942. She was assigned to Pan American Airways on July 2, 1942, for its Trans-African operations. She was apparently based at Accra (then Gold Coast, now Ghana). She was transferred to the Africa – Middle East Wing of the Air Transport Command on May 1, 1943. Her army serial number is 41-18401. The airplane was transferred to the French Air Force on November 20, 1945. She was finally transferred to the Israeli Air Self-Defense Force on January 25, 1967, and was assigned Israeli Air Force markings. This C-47 was the first cargo version of the DC-3 and has the large cargo doors, heavy floor, and tie downs for cargo. Since then she visits airshows to show what she looked like when she went to war in 1942. Her current owner is the Ozark Airlines Museum based in St. Charles, Missouri.

N33644: 1941 DC-3A-197E; c/n 4123. It was delivered as NC33644 in April 1941 to United Airlines. The aircraft was acquired by Weston Airlines in June 1942. In March 1958, the airplane was acquired by Hil-drown Venture, then re-registered as G-APKO by Shaikh Duajj Salman A Sabah on behalf of Trans Arabian. Later in 1958, the aircraft was acquired by Catalina Pacific, followed in subsequent years by California Airmotive Corp, Zantop Air Transport, J. Sorthun, P.L. Wilson and Universal Airlines. In 1972, it was purchased by Golden State Airlines, Inc., followed by Frontier Pacific Aircraft in 1979, and Southern Nevada Leasing Corporation in June 1980. The aircraft is currently owned by Michael Krimbrel, of Mason, New Hampshire and is dressed in Western Air Lines livery.

N341A: 1939 DC-3A-253A/C-41A; c/n 2145. She was delivered to the U.S. Army Air Force in September 1939 as 40-0070, assigned to First Staff Squadron and based at various airfields during the war. In December 1945, she was transferred to the Reconstruction Finance Corporation, and moved to Birmingham, Alabama. In July 1951, she was rebuilt by Stratomart, Inc. and registered as N4720V. In January 1952 she was sold to Superior Oil Company, and Pratt & Whitney R1830-94 engines were installed. In November 1952, she was sold to Ralph E. Fair of San Antonio and in November 1957, to Richfield Oil Co. and registered as N65R. In November 1966, she was registered as N598AR to Atlantic Richfield Co. of Philadelphia, Pennsylvania. In October 1970, she was sold to E.W. Brown of Orange, Texas, and registered as N32B. In February 1976, she went to Matilda Gray Stream of Orleans Parish, Lake Charles, Louisiana, and in March 1976, sold to Stream Aviation, Inc. In March 1978, she was sold to Huntsville Properties, in Huntsville, Texas. In April 1978, she went to Sun Belt Airways, also of Huntsville, and was registered as N132B and named *Tinsleys Boss*

Bird in October 1980. In May 1989, she was sold to Robert J. Pond, and registered as N132BP, and re-named *Miss Angela*. In March 1990, she was sold to Air Service, Inc. of Hockley, Texas, and in May 1993, sold to Rowan Drilling Co. of Houston, Texas and registered as N14RD. Registered as N341A, in November 2002, she was sold to her current owner, Legend Airways of Colorado LLC.

C-GDAK: 1939 C-47; c/n 2141. This C-47 was originally delivered to Eastern Airlines as NC1729, Fleet No. 347. The aircraft was acquired by the United States War Department in 1942 and flew as a C-49 until it was returned to Eastern Airlines in 1945. This aircraft served with Eastern until June 12, 1952, when it was sold to Purdue Aeronautics. North Central Airlines took over the aircraft on March 7, 1953, and operated it as Fleet No. 22. On November 30, 1964, the aircraft went to Houston Aviation Production Corporation and flew with Aircraft Charters, Inc. and Houston Aviation Production Corporation in Houston, Texas, until 1966. In 1968, the aircraft was acquired by the University of North Dakota in Grand Forks, North Dakota, until it was sold in 1972 to Shamrock Leasing, Inc. which operated the aircraft in Minnesota until 1979. In 1981, the Canadian Warplane Heritage Museum at the Hamilton International Airport in Mount Hope, Ontario, acquired the aircraft, where it underwent a 14-month major restoration before it flew again in June 1982. The aircraft has Wright Cyclone 1820-202A engines and has accumulated 81,499 flight hours.

N143D: 1938 DC-3A; c/n 2054, *Darla Dee*. Originally built at the Santa Monica factory and then flown to New York, she had her wings removed and was shipped to Fokker's facility in Belgium, and delivered to Swiss Air Lines as HB-IRO. After World War II, she came to the United States and was registered as N2817D. After a string of corporate owners, she was purchased by Ozark Airlines in 1962 and registered as N143D. In 1968, she was purchased by a cargo operation, and then by Academy Airlines in 1970. In 2001, she was bought by Gryder Networks LLC. In 2005, Herpa Miniature Models took up sponsorship of the airplane. She's currently based in Georgia.

N41HQ: 1938 C-41; c/n 2053. This is the only C-41 in the world. She was a DC-3 headed to United Air Lines, and General Henry "Hap" Arnold wanted one for the U.S. Army Air Corps. The exterior is polished aluminum and has the original markings. The interior is like a 1930s airliner. Her previous owner was Otis

Spunkmeyer Cookie Company, which took her to Normandy in 1994 as part of the 50th anniversary of the D-Day invasion. Her current owner is Jim Gabbert, and she's based at Metropolitan Oakland International, in California.

N18121: 1937 DC-3; c/n 1997. One of the oldest DC-3s still flying today and with more than 91,000 total airframe hours logged, she is also one of the highest-time aircraft in the world. She was based for many years at Vancouver, Washington's Pearson Field, which celebrated its 100th anniversary in 2005. She's owned by Blue Skies Air LLC, and based at Aurora, Oregon, and is undergoing further restoration.

N1934D: (not in formation) 1934 DC-2-118B; c/n 1368. She was originally delivered as NC14296 to Pan American Airways. She saw service in South America, first registered as XA-BJL, then LG-ACA, then TG-ACA, and then back to the United States where she ended up as N4867V, with Johnson Flying Service. She was bought by Douglas Historical Society in 1972 and used often by Douglas Aircraft Company for VIP flights and other events through 1985. She was sold and then donated to the Museum of Flight in Seattle in early 2000. She has been restored to flight status through donations by Clay Lacy Aviation and is currently owned by the Museum of Flight Foundation.

Author's Note: If the current owner or operator referenced the airplane as "she," that point of view was maintained in this accounting.

All data on aircraft taken from The Last Time website (www.thelasttime.org), author interviews with current owners, the Douglas Production List online (http://www.abcdlist.nl/maind.html), and the FAA registry.

Acknowledgments

"NO MAN ACCOMPLISHES ANYTHING worthwhile alone."

—Donald Wills Douglas, in his acceptance speech
for the Guggenheim Medal at the
Biltmore Hotel in New York, January 1940

My gratitude goes out to everyone who contributed their memories to this book.

My heartfelt thanks especially to...

Pat McGinnis, for pulling out a scrapbook and sending me home with a picture of Senior and Bar, and to Jim Turner, for your efforts to preserve DAC history.

Jim Douglas, for sharing your memories of sailing and fishing with your dad, as well as his practical jokes.

The C.R. Smith Museum, for preserving American Airlines' great heritage, so closely tied to the DC-3.

Kelly Owen, the Grey Eagle who opened the door and opened your AA logbook. I hope I drive so well when I'm in my 90s.

Jackson McGowen (posthumously) and Dale Berkihiser, for giving me a glimpse into early Douglas Aircraft Company days.

Marge Hogan Horning (posthumously), for sharing your memories of a happy time, and to Hugh Horning, for your enduring commitment to Marge.

Dell Johnson, for trusting me with precious mementos, and her son, a first officer for AA, who saw me studying DC-3 manuals on a flight to ATL and made the connection to his mother.

Bill Tinkler for his friendship and his passion for aviation history, and for the DC-3 flying tips: I won't forget to lock the tailwheel, Captain!

Emily Warner, Ed Leek, Paul Wiell, and Julie Clark, for sharing your memories and your path through the skies.

Jene McDonald (posthumously), for sharing what it meant to be only 19 years old and commanding a C-47 in wartime, and to Jack Jackson and Jack Rickel for taking me behind the lines.

Doug Millard, Elvin Jackson and Tom Gribble, for their tales of the -3 in the great state of Alaska, and Scott Thompson, for being a shepherd of FAA history.

Brooks Pettit and Scott Glover, and to all the DC-3 crews and volunteers at The Last Time for carrying on such an important mission.

Terry Swindle and Truitt Harper, for sharing the days in the life of a freight pilot.

Tom Horne, for sharing your father's story of flying the C-47 in World War II, and helping me to understand why my great-uncle never talked about flying the Hump.

Tom Haines, for saying yes to this one, and Mike Collins, for capturing it on film.

My friends in Engineering, Quality, Supply Chain, Production, Finance and Service on the Skycatcher Core Team at Cessna Aircraft Company, for your camaraderie and knowledge, for putting up with my history lessons and "sunshine" moments, and for giving me insight into everything that goes into making a great airplane.

Jack and Rose Pelton, for helping me understand what the DAC legacy is all about.

My DC-3 co-conspirators: Charlie Atterbury, for all of your sage advice, and Matt Metelak, for carrying on your family's tradition in such a cool way.

Dan Gryder, for the email that started this whole mess, and for doing the right thing.

My family, my sweetie Mike, and my Fred, the best dog on the planet.

About the Author

The author with
Douglas' "scrapbook."

JULIE BOATMAN FILUCCI has devoted her career to the aviation industry. At Jeppesen Sanderson, she contributed to the *Guided Flight Discovery* pilot training system and flight instructor renewal courses as a technical writer and editor. At the Aircraft Owners and Pilots Association, she lead the "Catch-A-Cardinal" sweepstakes aircraft restoration project and flew and reported on a wide variety of classic and new aircraft as technical editor for *AOPA Pilot* magazine. She currently works for Cessna Aircraft Company as the manager of the Cessna Pilot Center flight school affiliate network. She holds a flight instructor certificate and an airline transport pilot certificate with a Douglas DC-3 type rating. She's on the board of directors for Dress For Success Wichita, and volunteers for Women in Aviation International. She and her husband live in an airport community outside of Wichita, Kansas, with their canine children.